# FROM THE PROJECTS TO THE PRESIDENCIES

Those of us in education never know how profound an impact we have on others even when it isn't planned. Nichelle Cook was just six years old when she attended her first university commencement. When President Lyons walked out on the stage at Jackson State wearing an Elizabethan Tam, she asked her mother what he was wearing and what she would have to do to get one. After her mother explained what he was wearing, and the hard work that comes with it, she decided at that moment that she wouldn't stop working hard until she got one! After graduating from Spelman College, with honors, and Loyola University New Orleans College of Law, she ordered herself a "fuzzy hat."

# FROM THE PROJECTS TO THE PRESIDENCIES

My Journey to Higher Education Leadership

James E. Lyons Sr.

University Press of Mississippi / Jackson

*Margaret Walker Alexander Series in African American Studies*

The University Press of Mississippi is the scholarly publishing agency of
the Mississippi Institutions of Higher Learning: Alcorn State University,
Delta State University, Jackson State University, Mississippi State University,
Mississippi University for Women, Mississippi Valley State University,
University of Mississippi, and University of Southern Mississippi.

www.upress.state.ms.us

The University Press of Mississippi is a member
of the Association of University Presses.

This work depicts actual events as truthfully as recollection permits and/
or can be verified by research. The names and identifying details of some
individuals may have been changed to respect their privacy.

Library of Congress Cataloging-in-Publication Data

Names: Lyons, James E., Sr., author.
Title: From the projects to the presidencies :
my journey to higher education leadership / James E. Lyons Sr.
Other titles: Margaret Walker Alexander series in African American studies.
Description: Jackson : University Press of Mississippi, 2024. |
Series: Margaret Walker Alexander series in African American studies
Identifiers: LCCN 2023051406 (print) | LCCN 2023051407 (ebook) |
ISBN 9781496851444 (hardback) | ISBN 9781496851451 (epub) |
ISBN 9781496851468 (epub) | ISBN 9781496851475 (pdf) |
ISBN 9781496851482 (pdf)
Subjects: LCSH: Lyons, James E., Sr. | African American college presidents—
United States—Biography. | African American college administrators—
Biography. | African Americans—Education (Higher) |
College presidents—United States—Biography.
Classification: LCC E748.L96 A3 2024 (print) | LCC E748.L96 (ebook) |
DDC 378.73092 [B]—dc23/eng/20231211
LC record available at https://lccn.loc.gov/2023051406
LC ebook record available at https://lccn.loc.gov/2023051407

British Library Cataloging-in-Publication Data available

# DEDICATION

This book is dedicated to the memories of my mother, Dora Lyons; my grandmother, Lizzina Pittman; my father-in-law, William J. Massie; my mother-in-law, Freddie Massie; my sister, Katrina; my brother, George; Mr. George Woods Sr.; and Mr. David Tillery.

It is especially dedicated to my wife Joy, my sons James Jr., Jamal, and Jack, my grandchildren, nieces and nephews, daughters-in-law, sisters-in-law, brothers-in-law, aunts, uncles, and cousins.

# CONTENTS

# ACKNOWLEDGMENTS

How does one acknowledge everyone who, over the past seventy years, helped make this journey possible? When I was a child there were individuals in the neighborhood, in school, and in church who reminded me of the difference between right and wrong. Throughout high school and college there were teachers, staff members, and coaches who saw something in me and were supportive.

When I was a young professional, there were individuals, too many to name here, who helped shape my focus. All of my pastors have been influential in different ways. At each place of employment there were individuals who helped make the job doable and who helped lighten my load. That includes folks at the Fort Rodman Job Corps Center, in New Bedford, Massachusetts; my fellow Peace Corps Volunteers who served with me in Ecuador; Wagner Junior High School in Philadelphia; and the University of Connecticut where I directed the Afro-American Cultural Center. One of my former student workers at the Cultural Center, Clifton McKnight, continues to be a friend here in Georgia, and encouraged me to stick with this project. As I started working in senior leadership positions in higher education, there were always individuals who reported directly to me: office staff, faculty, and students who helped me and showed their support. This includes institutions such as Kentucky State University, Fayetteville State University, Barber-Scotia College, Delaware State University, Bowie State University, Jackson State University, California State University Dominguez Hills, Dillard University, the University of the District of Columbia, and Concordia College Alabama. I certainly must acknowledge former Maryland Governor Martin O'Malley and former Lt. Governor Anthony Brown for making me an essential part of their leadership team in the role of secretary of higher education. There were other individuals like Grammy nominee Rev. Wintley

Phipps, who opened my eyes to the importance of marketing and branding, and professor Nchor Okorn, whose entrepreneurial drive nearly resulted in my starting a new career in the international coffee business.

Closer to home, I would also like to acknowledge the many groups and organizations of which I have been a part over the years, and who have all been a part of my journey at one point or another. I would especially like to acknowledge my brothers in the Omega Psi Phi Fraternity, Inc., Sigma Pi Phi (Boule), Beta Sigma Gamma, and organizations such as the National Association for Equal Opportunity in Higher Education (NAFEO), the Thurgood Marshall College Fund, UNCF, ACE, AASCU, NAICU, the Registry, and AGB.

Over the years I cannot count the times someone has said, "You've got so many stories, you ought to write a book!" It probably would not have happened at all had it not been for the insistence of my wife Joy. She finally got my attention during the pandemic, when she pointed out that I had nowhere to go and nothing to do, so there was no excuse for not sitting down to write; and I did! Once I started to write and began asking questions, there were authors like Dr. Charlie Nelms, Dr. Lerita Coleman Brown, Rev. Bill Nelsen, Dr. Henry Tisdale, Mr. Ron Ancrum, Mr. Carnelious Jones, and Dr. Robert L. Shepard who gave me the benefit of their experience by making comments and suggestions. My sons Jimmy, Jamal, and Jack picked up where their mother left off and provided encouragement as I worked on the manuscript. My elementary school classmate, public housing neighbor, and friend for nearly seventy years, attorney Richard Freeman, encouraged me to write this book because it tells the story of our old neighborhood. I have challenged him to do the same.

Finally, I want to thank the personnel at the University Press of Mississippi for believing in this effort and hanging in there with me until the end.

FROM THE PROJECTS TO THE PRESIDENCIES

# Chapter 1

# IN THE BEGINNING

As an amateur history buff, I have always enjoyed reading about the so-called Great Migration of African Americans leaving the South and heading "up north." But it really wasn't until I read the book *The Warmth of Other Suns* by Isabel Wilkerson that it dawned on me that my story is indirectly a part of that migration. My own mother, who was tired of picking tobacco, decided that she too would leave the South (North Carolina) and head north to find a better life. In her late teens she did what so many others were doing, hitched a ride and went from Rocky Mount, North Carolina, to Newport News, Virginia. She stayed there for a while, but her friends who had gone to Detroit convinced her that there were a lot of employment opportunities in factories and automobile plants in this big urban city, so she decided to check it out. After a brief stay in Detroit, she concluded that the city was too big and too fast for a country girl like herself, so she headed where some other friends and relatives were located, New Haven, Connecticut. I can remember as a teenager, attending neighborhood picnics, hearing the person on the microphone ask, "How many of you are from North Carolina?" and the crowd would go wild! Many Black residents of Connecticut migrated from North Carolina.

Mom took a job in a local factory, which produced items for the war. She worked there for a while and then decided to take another job, which would impact our lives for years to come. She decided to do what so many other African American women were doing, working as housekeepers for white suburban families. These women would take the bus to the last stop inside the city limits and be met by the lady of the household and driven to her home in the suburbs. This job worked out quite well because she worked there for more than twenty years. From time to time, when I needed some money, I would go with mom and do odd jobs such as raking leaves and painting the walkway leading to the house. There were times I was convinced they were creating jobs just so I could earn a little extra cash. I never heard my mom complain about money; she just worked hard every day to take care of her invalid mother and three children.

I was born in New Haven, and from birth until I was ten years old, we lived on the top floor of a very badly maintained tenement house. Six of us lived in a three-room apartment: my mother, grandmother, sister, brother, and my brother's father. There was a hole in the ceiling of our apartment, and from time to time a rat would fall down on our bed. So, none of us (me, my sister, or my brother) wanted to sleep on the side beneath the hole. As the oldest child I agreed to sleep on that side of the bed, but my sister and brother had to pay me when they had candy or soda! That worked out very well for me. There was such extreme poverty in the neighborhood that the local members of the Communist Party targeted our families. Oscar and his friends were very nice to all of us. I do not remember them trying to indoctrinate my mother or grandmother, perhaps other than through kindness. They would bring us groceries every holiday and gave puppies and kittens to some of the children. My brother and sister and I agreed to ask Oscar to bring us a Dalmatian puppy, which he agreed to do. We were so eager to have a puppy that we went out and found a dog's bed that had been discarded. I was chosen to fix it up. We could not agree on a name for our new puppy, so we agreed that we might have to name it "Puppy." A couple of months later we were still waiting for Oscar. He had never been away from us that long. I told a neighbor that Oscar had promised to give us a Dalmatian but we had not seen him in a while. The neighbor told us that the Communists would not be coming into our neighborhood anymore because the local Mafia beat them up and threatened to do more if they came back. That was the end of Oscar and our Dalmatian.

As a nine-year-old child I did hear people in the neighborhood referring to the Communists, and the Mafia, but those terms didn't mean anything to me. For all I knew at the time, they may have been social clubs. However, I was aware of the racial and ethnic differences. Our neighborhood was considered an Italian neighborhood. I knew what Italians looked like and that some spoke a different language. I enjoyed watching the men play Bocce ball. It was a very popular game that I would never see again until I visited some friends of mine while in college. While the men played Bocce ball they would buy clams on the half shell, pour hot sauce on them, and then swallow them raw. There were a couple of old men who used to rub my head for good luck, and if I did not protest, they would offer me the raw clams. To this day I enjoy eating raw clams on the half shell.

There were also a number of African American and Portuguese families in the neighborhood. In fact, our janitor/rent man was Portuguese. When we made a mess in the hallway, he would curse at us in a language we could not understand. So, at a very early age I was exposed to a strong multicultural environment. I have been told that I probably developed my love for foreign languages as a young child, given the fact that every day I heard people speaking in Portuguese and Italian. Our elementary school was the Hamilton Street School, formerly a Catholic School called St. Patrick's Elementary School. The city school district was transitioning our school from parochial to public. While I was there the principal was a nun. She wore a thick leather strap on her waist to be used on anyone who got out of line. I learned three very important things at that time. Don't mess around with Sister Edmunds because she would use the strap on you and then send a note home to tell your parents what she had done. You were required to have it signed to prove that your parents had seen it. I only had to take a note home one time because my grandmother spanked me for getting spanked in school. The second thing that I learned at this time is that I had health issues.

I learned at a young age that I had a health condition that set me apart from most of the other children in kindergarten. I had what was called a functional heart murmur. Every child who had a health issue had to take cod-liver oil daily, and we had to take a one-hour nap. Most of the other children teased us because we took a nap every day in school. I really did not understand what a heart murmur was, but it would later come back to haunt me. A third thing that I learned early on was that I had a sufficient level of intelligence in the first grade that caused my teacher to suggest that I be moved from the afternoon to the morning section. The morning first-grade class was considered the smarter of the two classes; it did not take long for us to figure that out. When a student in the morning section moved out of town, I was one of the afternoon students who was being considered as a replacement. I was too young to understand the process, but it involved having my mother get dressed up and come to our school to discuss the move. I was not selected to move to the morning section, and nobody ever said another word about it, including my mom. However, I was eavesdropping and heard someone in the room criticizing the way my mother was dressed, and that same person said that we lived in the tenement!

I enjoyed Hamilton Street School especially when we were allowed to come to school late in order to get ashes, or because it was a holy day. Once I do remember being asked by the principal why I was late, and I responded that I had to go get ashes and had until 10:00 a.m. to arrive in school. She told me that she had met my mother and that I was Pentecostal. But she could see that I had ashes on my forehead, so she just laughed and sent me to my room. I took advantage of every opportunity to arrive late to school on religious holidays. Of course, I did the same thing in junior high school when there was a Jewish holiday.

One afternoon when I arrived home, my mother told me that we were moving to the other side of town, and this would be my last week at Hamilton Street School. She said that I could not even mention it to my brother's dad, who was now living with us. The housing authority had very strict rules about who could stay in their facility because the monthly rent was based on the income of the renter. When the renter was a female and family, and no male was listed, rumor had it that the housing authority sent staff to the apartment to try and "catch" a male living there. If it could be proven that the person was indeed living there in violation of the policy, the renter would be evicted. Some males chose to live nearby in order to keep the rent as low as possible. This often resulted in the unintended consequence of children growing up without a male figure in the home. My mother explained that she was moving so that we would have a better home and therefore a better life. Even though it was the projects, it was 100 percent better than what we had. We would now have a shower and bathtub, and my sister and grandmother would have their own room, as would my brother and I. Mom had already ordered bunk beds and kitchen furniture, which suggested that she had been working on this move for a couple of months. Early on a Thursday morning she told me to say goodbye to my teachers because that would be my last day in this school and in this neighborhood. I hated to say goodbye to the teachers and my friends, but I had no choice. I did not like the idea of moving in the middle of the year, but that is what we did. Little did I know that I would end up in the same class with a few of these kids when I entered high school.

In some ways, moving to the projects made me feel like the people on the television show *The Jeffersons*; we were moving on up! The housing authority provided a stove and a refrigerator. We now had walls and a ceiling without holes, a shower and bathtub, and windows without lead paint. I have often thanked God that we didn't eat enough lead paint while living in the tenement to get sick! We had a basketball goal behind our building, there was grass around the house, and some of our North Carolina neighbors attempted to grow collard greens in a garden, right there in the projects. To make us feel better about the move, my mother gave us a cat, our first! She was jet black, so we named her Black Gal. It was a nice gesture on her part, but it didn't change the fact that we made an abrupt move in the middle of the school year, much to my displeasure.

When I went to my new elementary school, Winchester School, I was in for a real surprise. Nearly all of the students were Black, which reflected my new neighborhood; most of my teachers were Black, and the principal was a Black man! Winchester School was not Hamilton Street School, so I had to adjust quickly, and I did. I really got involved at Winchester and soon became known like I had been there six years rather than six months. At the beginning of my sixth-grade year I was made aware of an opportunity called the Ulysses S. Grant Program. Each elementary school with a large Black student population nominated two students at the end of the sixth grade to participate. If accepted, they were to be tutored by Yale University students after school for two years. If they successfully completed the program, they would be admitted to one of the elite prep schools to begin the ninth grade. I could only dream of attending Choate, Loomis, Taft, or Hotchkiss. It was an outstanding program, and I was honored to be one of the students under consideration. When I learned that I was not one of the two students nominated by Winchester School, I asked the principal about it. He said that the only reason I was not one of the two was because I was new to the school and the committee felt that it would be unfair to select the new student! This was a one-time consideration, so I could not be considered the following year. This was one of the first major disappointments that I experienced in life, but it didn't deter me from attempting to take advantage of other opportunities to improve myself. Two of my closest friends, to this day, happened to have been selected for the program. One went to Hotchkiss and the other attended Taft. They are both proud of what we have each accomplished, and we enjoy telling people how long we have been friends.

New Haven, Connecticut, was an interesting place to grow up. Situated between New York City and Boston, it gave us the best and the worst of those two metropolitan areas. I can remember friends taking the train to those two cities to see a play, visit a museum, or attend a concert. I can also remember them taking a train to New York City to bring back drugs. I took the train to go to Brooklyn Dodgers' baseball games with our coach. New Haven itself was a military-industrial city, with Yale University sitting right downtown. Yale was also the buffer between the various ethnic communities, African American, Jewish, and Italian. As a result of the presence of Yale, a lot of things happened in the city, both good and bad. We took advantage of many of the things that went on. For example, the trial of Black Panther Bobbie Seale took place in New Haven. On the day that the verdict was rendered I will always remember the show of force put on by law enforcement. Every law-enforcement officer in Connecticut must have been activated and in New Haven that day in anticipation of a guilty verdict. There was a real fear that people would destroy New Haven. I remember standing out in front of the courthouse in May of 1971 when the judge declared a mistrial. It was indeed a fair outcome for many who had lived in fear of what might happen if he had been found guilty.

There was another event that took place in downtown New Haven that drew the attention of people from all over Connecticut and the surrounding area. Senator John F. Kennedy had declared that he was running for president and scheduled an appearance in downtown New Haven. People came from all over the state to see the senator from our neighboring state, Massachusetts. Having the opportunity to walk downtown to the Green and listen to Senator Kennedy made us all feel proud. There was no doubt in anyone's mind that the presence of Yale University was attractive to those planning the senator's schedule. This event had much greater significance for me because it was the day that I met a young girl who would later become my wife. I was standing on the corner when she walked by headed to see Senator Kennedy. I spoke to her as she walked past, and then I turned to a friend of mine and joked, "I think I am going to marry that girl!"

New Haven also attracted the attention of Malcolm X, the now famous African American Muslim minister. He decided to open a mosque directly across the street from the projects where I lived. Initially it was open to the public, so my girlfriend and I used to go to the building every week and listen to him. He enjoyed debating scholars from Yale. Historians, economists, political scientists, and religious scholars, Black and white, would challenge him, but would never prevail. Even the scholars, many of whom disagreed with his program, had to acknowledge his brilliance as a debater. The reality about New Haven was that even Yale could not keep urban specialists from recognizing the fact that even those of us who lived in the shadows of one of the greatest universities in the world were really a part of one of the worst urban neighborhoods in the city and the state.

Chapter 2

# HOW CAN YOU LIVE LIKE THIS?

One of the most haunting questions ever put to me in my life came from one of my junior high school classmates. I had been invited to visit their homes on several occasions and enjoyed the conversations. One of the things that stood out immediately is the fact that these seventh- and eighth-grade boys were already talking about college. Most of them already knew where they were going to apply, and some had sent for and received a college catalog. Education was a very high priority for their parents as well. No such conversations were taking place in my neighborhood. So, in a very naïve way, I concluded that the only reason my white classmates possessed so many material things was education. To me it seemed as though the more education they had, the more they enjoyed the finer things of life! As a seventh grader I did not understand the full socioeconomic issue of race and racism in America. All I knew was what I could see, and so at a very early stage in my life I concluded that if I wanted to compete with my white classmates, and have what they had, I needed to get as much education as possible; and that meant at least a high school diploma.

After visiting their homes a couple of times, I decided to invite them to my home in the projects. They seemed quite eager to visit me and as one said "have a new experience." To be honest I was surprised that they took me up on my invitation because when their parents heard that they were going to Dixwell Avenue to a friend's house, I am sure there was a lot of conversation. The only positive things that many white folks knew about Dixwell Avenue was that a singing group named the Five Satins had a hit song called "In the Still of the Night." They started their singing career in our neighborhood. The other positive thing was that I lived just a few blocks from Yale. What I would learn a decade later was that their parents did talk and decided that if all four of them were going together it would be alright.

And just as my mother would lecture us about how to act in North Carolina because the South was different and white folks expected you to "stay in your place," their parents gave them a similar lecture about how they should act going to the "Hood." The visit was very interesting because they didn't know what to expect and I didn't either. That afternoon we walked from the school to the projects the same route that I took every day. The first thing that was obvious to them was that they were the only white kids walking in this direction. One of the first questions that came up was "don't any white people live near you?" As we approached my building, one of them said, "I thought we were going to your home?" "This is my home, the Elm Haven Housing Project at 145 Dixwell Avenue," was my reply.

After meeting my grandmother and having a slice of sweet potato pie, we went outside and walked around. I had not intended to give them a guided tour, but I was proud of my neighborhood and wanted them to see that everyone did not live like they did, but I was happy. Some of my friends who were sitting on "Wine Rock," a name that it was given for obvious reasons, yelled "are y'all planning to move to the projects?" We all had a good laugh about that as they quickly responded no! The local "wine head," about whom I will say more later, asked if they had some spare change because he was hungry. They each gave him some change. I showed them my elementary school, my storefront church, and the laundromat where we washed and dried our clothes on days when we couldn't hang them outdoors. When I explained to them that nobody in our building had a washing machine, they couldn't believe it. I took them into a small convenience store where the only real business was the numbers racquet. They had heard that you could play the numbers each day, but it was illegal, and controlled by the Mafia. You could purchase a book of dreams that would give you a number for each dream. It was not uncommon to be asked "what did you dream last night?" We walked around and ran into a couple of people that they knew from school. We had a very good time. As they prepared to head back to their homes, one of them asked me, after declaring that he meant no disrespect, "Lyons, how can you live like this?"

This question rang in my ears for years. On the one hand, I acknowledged that it was coming from a seventh grader who was a friend, and should be viewed as such; however, on another level it was very profound. As a seventh grader he considered himself a friend of mine. We liked each other, we attended the same classes, participated in the same after-school activities, from time to time did homework together, and yet he lived on Chapel Street and I on Dixwell Avenue, and they were like two different worlds. There were a lot of things about my neighborhood that I did not like, but it was *my* neighborhood. Yes, the heroin addicts sat out on Wine Rock drinking wine every day. We all knew that they had to steal a certain number of items each day and sell them to feed their drug habit; but they were my friends and former classmates and my neighbors. I often tell people today that the drug addicts in my neighborhood had a value system that doesn't necessarily exist today. For example, they respected their elders, so if they were about to shoot up and my mother walked by, someone would say, "Hold up, here comes Miss Dora." I can remember being asked by one of them, when I was away in college, if he could meet my mother after church on Sunday night and walk her home. He told me that the young junkies didn't respect their elders and my mother was not safe walking from church at night; and of course, he wanted to get paid. For me, it was worth giving him a few dollars when I came home for the weekend. I knew that I was helping to feed his drug habit, but my mother's safety was more important to me. She could now walk home from church at night without fear of being assaulted.

We had more than our share of neighbors with alcohol dependency issues. Some of them were able to function quite well. I worked in a factory with a man who was drunk the entire weekend. On Monday morning however, he would get up and drive us to work, and he was sober. He and several others who worked with us would cash their weekly paycheck in the liquor store and sit in the car and drink until they were drunk. I watched a couple of them spend their entire paycheck on alcohol and then stagger home drunk and broke. I suggested to their girlfriends and wives that they go to a certain store each Friday afternoon and take the check before they spent it all on alcohol. They appreciated my suggestion and started doing so. There was one person, whom we called a wino, who was very "special." Both my mother and grandmother advised me to stay away from him, but

I didn't listen because this wino actually had something to say to us young boys. His name was "Get Out the Car."

My mother and grandmother claimed that during a cold winter night he fell asleep in someone's car. The next morning the owner opened his car door and upon seeing a man in it he said, "Get out the car." During the frigid winter months, they claim he would commit a petty crime and when he stood before the judge, he would act disrespectfully and be held in contempt of court. His purpose was to be sentenced to at least ninety days so that he could spend the winter in jail and not out on the street. Whenever he saw us, he would say "what you say Rolla?" "Do you want to hear my poem?" We would pool our change and give it to him and then sit down on the ground in front of him as though he were a great philosopher. Every day he would repeat the same verse to us:

> When I was down and didn't have a penny, all my friends I didn't have any but when I began to rise and get on my feet, all these friends I began to meet up came Joe and Bill and Jackson, they said hello Get Out, can you give us a dime? I said hello fellas I ain't seen you in a long, long time. And before you get ONE cent from me in this fix you will have to be . . . so blind and crippled you cannot see and both feet cut off up above your knee. Because I tell you guys beyond a reasonable doubt, don't nobody know you when you're down and out!

Before going into the store to buy his bottle of wine he would tell us that he is a college graduate who came on hard times and he did not want us to be like him. So, he cautioned us about alcohol, he cautioned us about the meaning of friendship, and he cautioned us about how to deal with women. I did not expect my mother to understand why I listened to him so often; I didn't fully understand it myself. What I knew was that I was intrigued by the fact that a wino cared enough about us to give us advice so we could avoid his mistakes. I, for one, took it to heart. During my career I have given many speeches in which I recited this poem. It has been, by far, the most requested information that has come out of my mouth! One of my secretaries used to keep copies of it available to respond to the many requests.

And yes, I was one of a few young men in my neighborhood who had not been in jail, and I was teased about it. One of my friends was already an accomplished thief by the age of sixteen and expected to spend his life in and out of jail. One afternoon he called me over to Wine Rock and asked me if I needed any shirts. I told him that I did, but I did not want him to steal something just for me. He then showed me a floor plan of several stores downtown, and indicated where the shelves were that contained shirts in my size. He noted that in two of the stores, everyone went to the back at noon for lunch, and that was the best time to enter the store. I thanked him for sharing the information and went on about my business because I had no interest in stealing shirts. While in high school I had an experience that was quite upsetting. Someone broke into the laundromat and stole the change machine that was on the wall. When the police asked if anyone had information about the break-in, they were told that Jimmy Lyons did it. The detectives who visited our home asked me where I was during the time of the break-in. I reported that I was with our pastor on a trip to Mount Vernon, New York. My pastor confirmed my alibi and the detectives apologized and asked, "Why would your friends blame you?" I replied, "Because they wanted me to get in trouble like them."

At a very young age I couldn't help but notice the number of female-headed households in my neighborhood. Some were the result of teenage pregnancies and some were not. But the impact was that a disproportionate number of us were growing up without our fathers in the home and I felt that was not a positive thing, even though mothers, like my own, worked extremely hard to provide for us. I can remember a group of us discussing the idea of starting a club called "I don't know who my Daddy is." After discussing the large potential membership, and how much we could collect in dues payments, we decided against the idea and kind of laughed it off. While I laughed off the idea of forming an organization, I was quite concerned about the impact that this was having on the Black families in my neighborhood. I could already see that in far too many cases, young girls were following in their mothers' footsteps and having babies out of wedlock. It was clear to me that this was becoming a generational issue because we had neighbors where the grandmother, mother, and now daughters all had their children out of wedlock. I was too young to understand the sociology of all of this, but I did see that things were different when I went to visit my Jewish friends. Every one of them lived with both parents. From time to time, they would ask me about my family, and I surprised them talking about how happy we were as a family. The question "how could I live like this" evoked serious responses that I internalized. I loved my neighborhood and the people who lived there. There were problems and there were issues. We may not have had much but we did the best we could with what we had. We had a value system in place, such that parents were not afraid to discipline another person's child if it was warranted. They might even spank you and then tell your mother that they did it. We didn't have much, but my mother would sweep the hallway with ammonia so that the winos would not sleep there. There was a strong work ethic among most of the women. Many of them, like my mother, took the bus out to the suburbs where they "did house work" for white families. What was amazing to me was that after working in another person's house all day, they came home at night and took care of us! I was proud of my neighborhood, and even years later when I was interviewed by a television network, I talked about Dixwell Avenue. Years later I took my sons back to Dixwell Avenue, and one of my classmates was out on the street. He was a Vietnam vet who returned to New Haven addicted to heroin. He told my sons that the homeboys were proud of their dad because he never turned his back on them. They had seen me on television and read some of the interviews, and I always spoke proudly of Dixwell Avenue and the Elm Haven Housing Project. Years later when they demolished Elm Haven, my friends saved me a brick from building 145, because they knew I would cherish the memory. I had it mounted while I was president of California State University, Dominguez Hills.

During my ninth-grade year in junior high school, the local board of education decided to change the school boundary lines, which had a significant impact on everyone in my neighborhood. For decades, everyone in our neighborhood who attended high school went to Hillhouse High School. It was a tradition that was very important. However, the new school boundary was right along Dixwell Avenue. Everyone on the odd number side of the street would now go to Wilbur Cross High School. I lived at 145 Dixwell, so I was now going to Cross rather than Hillhouse. The reason we were given for the change was that the mayor of New Haven was receiving accolades from around the country for his urban renewal agenda, yet it was pointed out to him that the two high schools in town were segregated. Jewish students and African American students attended Hillhouse, and Italian students attended Wilbur Cross. This wasn't news to anyone; it had been like that for years. So why change it now? There was a lot of negative reaction in the communities. Those of us scheduled to attend Wilbur Cross who had already begun making plans to attend Hillhouse were devastated. We decided that as a show of solidarity we would ride the bus on the first day of school, and then walk from the second day forward. I could walk to Hillhouse in ten minutes; now I was being asked to ride a bus. Walking to Wilbur Cross was the first time I engaged in a formal protest. It took us forty-five minutes to walk to school, but we were trying to make a statement.

When we arrived at Wilbur Cross the first day, you would have thought we were Martians descending from the sky. The white students and teachers were either outside or peering through the windows. The truth is that Wilbur Cross had never experienced that many Black students entering the building at one time since its founding. It was clear to everyone that we really were not welcome. The Italian students felt threatened, and we felt like aliens. The first few weeks there were fights every day between Black and Italian students. Even in some of the classrooms the teachers showed their displeasure. One of my teachers assigned the girls to sit on one side of the room, and the boys on the other. One of my classmates asked the teacher if this was being done to keep the Black boys from sitting close to the white girls. He did not respond. I was in the academic prep sections and got along well in the classrooms; but once I entered the hallway, it seemed like a different school. The daily fighting continued, and it often led to suspensions. The daily school notice listed the suspensions, and it was almost laughable when you saw who was suspended, Cavalotto and Chapman; Cicarella and Charles; and Piscitelli and Dixon. Everyone in the school knew what was going on. Unfortunately, the fighting continued until the start of football and indoor track practice. We realized that we would have to find a way to work together in order to be successful on the field. As student athletes became friendlier, the daily fighting between Blacks and Italians ceased. I was on the track team and had a good relationship with the other members of the team. At the beginning of the school year students walked through the halls in groups, based on their race. By the time track season began, the members of the track team walked together. We were setting the example!

The most important thing that happened to me at Wilbur Cross High School was the fondness that I developed for Miss Deegan, who taught Spanish and French. In fact, I would have to identify her as one of the teachers who had the greatest impact on my life. She was a tough teacher, and everyone knew that. But if you were interested in really trying to learn Spanish or French, she was your ally and your advocate. She didn't care about your race or gender or whether you lived on the other side of town. If you enjoyed studying a foreign language and worked hard to satisfy the requirements of her course, she was your friend. It was because of her that I decided to continue studying Spanish in high school and in college. What started out as the worst possible high school scenario became a blessing to me going forward. She became a personal reference for me, the first teacher that I asked to do so. She wrote reference letters for me until I completed college. That is how strong a bond we developed.

# Chapter 3

# UCONN

## Arrived Naked, Left Fully Robed

There were three factors that led to my decision to apply to college even though we had no money. First, the desire to continue studying Spanish was the major factor. I enjoyed studying a foreign language, and knew that if I attended college, I could pursue my interest. Even my classmates enjoyed my enthusiasm for the study of Spanish and French. Some of them started calling me Señor Lyons instead of Jim. The second factor was the indirect influence of my Jewish friends. Although they did not attend Wilbur Cross High School, I remained in touch with most of them. By the end of my junior year, all of them had started the application process. That was not the case in my high school. We eventually were contacted by a counselor, but it was not the highest priority at my school. So, I reasoned that I ought to do like them.

The third and final reason that I applied to college was the pressure that I felt from my girlfriend's father. The young woman that I met on the way to see then-Senator John F. Kennedy was now my girlfriend. For that reason, I have no doubt that her father wanted any boy who was visiting his daughter to have a certain level of seriousness about his future. One indication of that seriousness was applying to college. Many of my friends teased me about dating the daughter of the most prominent Black physician in town. They would often ask, "Does he know you live in the projects?" Or, "Does he know you are from the hood?" When I went to her home, which was three blocks outside of the city limits, I used to hitchhike. Everyone knew that when they saw me hitchhiking, I was probably going to see my girlfriend. I never had a problem getting a ride because people wanted to be helpful. Even the driver of the city bus would sometimes let me ride for free because he knew where I was going. Although her dad and I talked about a host of things, the conversation always got back to college, and my future plans. It didn't take long for me to realize that if I were going to have these conversations, they needed to be real. The best way to do that was to apply to college.

Soon I began writing to colleges to request a catalog and an application. I was a solid "B Average" student in high school so I figured that somebody would admit me whether I had the money to attend or not. That allowed me to say to her father that I had applied to the University of Connecticut, Howard University, Syracuse University, Trinity College, and Central Connecticut State College. There was no doubt in my mind that the hard work that I had put in, and the encouragement of my mother to graduate from high school, had paid off in the end. My first acceptance was from UConn. When I opened the letter, I was so excited that I fell on the floor kicking and screaming. My grandmother thought that I was having some kind of seizure. She yelled, "Are you alright?" My girlfriend's father was also pleased with my choice of colleges, and the fact that I had at least one acceptance. I felt that the pressure was off and I could now sit back and enjoy my final year in high school. I had been following advertisements in the local newspaper about college loans and decided to ask my mother if she would consider going to our local bank and applying for one. They made it sound like the process was very simple. It seemed you simply went to the bank and told them how much you needed, and they would write you a check. Mom agreed to go to the bank, which was a few blocks down the street, and complete the loan application process. For the first time I allowed myself to really get serious about going away to college. What happened next was a real game changer.

Given that the bank was not far from the projects, I stopped by one afternoon after school. The staff person asked when my mother and I could return to the bank. I was so excited that I told her we would be there the following day, without discussing it with my mother. I ran home and told my mother that the bank was ready for us to return and discuss the student loan. We returned to the bank the next day, and much to our surprise we were told that the loan was not approved. Needless to say, I was crushed. When I asked why the loan was not approved, we were told that the bank needed collateral, and my mother didn't have any. I responded that the advertisement in the newspaper didn't say anything about needing collateral! I really wanted to do something crazy like take the branch manager hostage and tell them to call the newspaper and the police department. I would tell the newspaper that the ad for the student loan program didn't say that you had to be rich in order to get a loan. I would tell the newspaper that this is an outrage. If you are Black, poor, live in the projects, and your mother does housework, you cannot go to college. Instead, I told the staff person that the ad was misleading and that the bank's interest was making money and not assisting people to go to college. I did not want to go to jail, nor did I want any of the colleges that had admitted me to rescind my admission because I was crazy. So, we left the bank and headed home. My mother was disappointed, but not in the same way that I was. Given the reality of our situation, it was probably not the first time that she had been turned down for a loan. This experience at the bank was really an eyeopener. I suddenly realized that one of the main reasons that so many of the young people in my neighborhood did not go on to college was that they simply didn't have the resources to do so. It really wasn't because they had no desire to go to college nor because they lacked ambition. It took money, and most of us didn't have any!

The bank's denial of the student loan was not only crushing to me personally, but it led to an action on my part that I have second guessed my entire life. When my mother and I returned home from the bank I was furious. Furious at the bank for what I considered to be misleading advertising, and furious at the father that I had never known. I told my sister, who was two years younger than me, what had happened at the bank and that I was going to call our father and let him know that he had a responsibility to help my mother send me to college. I really didn't know who my father was, but I was going to take a chance and call a certain household. I had always been curious about a woman who brought us gifts on our birthdays, at Easter, and at Christmas. We knew that she lived with her son and his family but not much more than that. Neither my mother nor my maternal grandmother, who lived with us, ever talked about her other than to say that she was a nice lady. On one occasion we secretly followed her to find out where she lived. Much to our surprise she lived five blocks from us. If this "mysterious" woman was our paternal grandmother, then the reality was that her son was our father and he lived just five blocks away. How could a man live five blocks from his children and never contact them? I was so angry that I decided to call the telephone number of the mystery woman. A woman answered the phone, whose voice I did not recognize. When I asked, "May I speak to my father please?" she said that I had the wrong number. I told her that I had the correct number and wanted to speak with him. I told her that if he wasn't available ask him to return the call to his son. I asked, "Please tell him that his son is trying to go to college, and needs his help, okay?" That was the end of the call, and I didn't really expect that he would return the call. In fact, nothing happened for a few days, and I concluded that perhaps I had been wrong about the entire ordeal. About four days later that changed.

When I arrived at home from school my grandmother verbally attacked me like she had never done before. She told me that I had hurt my mother so badly that she was sick. She asked, "How could you do this to your mother?" I went into her bedroom, and she was sitting on the side of her bed crying. At that point it became clear I had "opened some old wounds" that were so painful that it left my mother crying like I had never seen before. I will always remember her words: "So, Mister Man, you thought that you were grown?" She went on to tell me that she had received a call from my father, and he threatened to have her locked up for attempting to destroy his marriage. He believed that she asked me to call him about college and repeated that he still did not want to have anything to do with her or "her children." I could have been angry with my father and gone to his house, but that was not my concern. My concern was that I had hurt my mother so badly after all that she had done for me. I apologized to her as best as a seventeen-year-old could and promised never to do anything like that again. Keeping the close relationship with my mother was more important to me than attempting to develop a relationship with someone that I didn't know. Neither of us ever mentioned this incident again. In my mind, I no longer had a father.

Coming to the conclusion that I really didn't have a father was not as easy as it sounds. Of course, I knew that I had a father biologically, but he was not someone that I could approach. I had never seen him or spoken to him, so in a very real way he did not exist. I vowed that I would never hurt my mother like this again. The next time that I mentioned my father was as an adult. I was interested in the idea of tracing my African roots, and the organization behind it requested a DNA sample and asked questions about my father. When I mentioned this project to my mother and asked where my father was from, she said Philadelphia. That was all she would say. The final time I asked her a question about my father was when I was diagnosed with prostate cancer and the oncologist was asking questions about my family history regarding health concerns. She did not respond and that was it!

Over the years I have moved on from where I was as a young adult. However, having no knowledge of my father has been an issue for me in two ways. First, it has been quite embarrassing over the years to have to tell someone that "I don't know anything about my father." Some people have looked at me in disbelief before moving on with their questions; and others found a way of moving ahead with the questions without drawing attention to my answer. From time to time, usually in a health-related conversation with a physician, the question has been repeated, "You don't know anything about your father?" Of course, I understood why this question was being asked, but my answer was the same: "No I don't, can we move on?" The second reason that I have felt bad about this situation is because I have not been able to be responsive to my sons. When they were old enough to understand what was happening, they would ask me how I felt, especially around Father's Day. They wanted to be good sons, and they were, but they wondered how I felt celebrating the day with them, never having been able to experience it from the son's point of view. Every year I assured them that I was okay. What I regret to this day is the fact that they will never know one side of their family history. They were blessed to have spent time with and enjoyed three of their grandparents, and they know it. I have told them that with my father living just five blocks from where I grew up, it is possible that their paternal grandfather saw us, even though we have never seen him! I have always thanked God that I did not allow this situation to ruin my life. In fact, it may even have made me stronger and more determined to succeed.

Having ruled out the idea of going to college because we did not have the money, I decided to do what several of my Black classmates had done and visit the Air Force recruitment office. There really wasn't anything wrong with the Air Force. After speaking with several other guys who were also considering it, I decided that it would be the best thing for me. I could leave home, travel around the world, start a career that I could continue after the military, and still have money for college. I decided not to discuss my decision to join the Air Force with anyone outside of the family, not even my girlfriend. As far as the outside world knew, I was probably going to UConn. In fact, my high school yearbook had a lot of "Good luck at UConn" wishes from other members of the senior class. Little did they know that I had done everything to enter the military but take the physical examination. It was difficult pretending that I was going to college, especially when my favorite teachers initiated a discussion. But I really could not tell anyone that I worked hard, got decent grades, applied, and was admitted to college, but didn't have any money beyond what I made shining shoes and delivering newspapers. I would later learn as an adult that what I experienced was not uncommon. Many poor children, who have the aptitude but don't have the money, never make it to college.

What made things even more painful was the fact that UConn began sending me information that went out to all the incoming students. They even started calling us the graduating Class of 1965. I responded when necessary and threw the other stuff away. On the day before freshmen were to arrive on campus, Mrs. G., my mother's boss, asked her if I needed a ride to the campus. She knew that my mother did not have a car, and given that she would be driving her niece there, I could ride with them. My mother responded that I was not going to college because she did not have the money. I will always believe that at that point Mrs. G. realized that there was no way that Dora could have saved money for her son to go to college because she wasn't paid that much. According to my mother, Mrs. G. told her to get me ready for college and she would pick me up in the morning. She asked that my mother not mention it to anyone, including her husband. When my mother arrived at home, she told me that I was going to college and that her boss was paying. After thanking Jesus for touching Mrs. G.'s heart, I began preparation to go to college in the morning. It didn't take much to prepare because all I had was a blue cord suit, a sweatshirt, and a pair of khaki pants that looked good enough to take with me. The next morning the car pulled up in front of the projects, and everyone outside on the street wondered who the white lady was that drove away with me. Years later I would tell them the story.

When we arrived at the registrar's office at UConn, we were told that they could not find my records because they didn't think I was going to enroll that semester. Mrs. G. assured them that I was there to register and that she had the payment for a full year. Once all the payment matters were completed, I was assigned to Tolland Hall in the "jungle" on North Eagleville Road. All the male students lived in the "jungle," and at times we probably behaved like animals in the jungle, thus the nickname. I was full of excitement, and it showed. I didn't need help with my belongings because I only had one bag. I thanked her again for all that she had done for me and told her that I would keep in touch. After some small talk with the resident advisors, I made it to my room on the top floor. My roommate was not there yet, so I was able to choose the bed and the desk that I wanted. I remember lying across the bed and looking up at the ceiling and asking myself, "What the hell am I doing here?" Why would I put myself in a position to be ridiculed because I was poor and felt out of place? The fact that my mother had to find a ride and bring me some clothes to wear would have discouraged some people. So why was I there, and what was I doing?

The truth is that in my heart I believed that I had every right to be there. The fact that I was Black and poor did not deter me. Also, there were people who believed in me like my mother, Mrs. G., Miss Deegan, and people in my church. The fact that Mrs. G. went into her pocket and paid for my first year in college is something I will never forget. She didn't have to do it! One weekend I surprised my family by returning home on a Saturday morning. But when I got there my grandmother told me that mom was working that day and would not be home until late. They were having a dinner party and she was working. When I asked why she was working on the weekend after having worked all week, my grandmother said that she was trying to pay back the money that we were "given" for me to attend the university. To say that I became angry would be an understatement. I kept asking myself, "Why would Mrs. G. do this?" When my mother returned home late that evening, I decided not to discuss the matter. I focused, instead, on the fact that a classmate had to drive home for a banquet and asked me if I wanted to ride with him. He was from West Haven, Connecticut, and said that he had no problem dropping me off and picking me up Sunday afternoon. I thought that it would be a nice surprise.

By the time I returned to campus Sunday afternoon, I had already decided that I would earn some money and send it home so that mom could pay off "our debt." When some of the guys in my dormitory saw that I could starch and iron my blue jeans, they asked if I would do theirs. Soon I had a small business going in my room. Thanks to my mother I knew how to iron, so it became a source of extra money. On trips back home I would bring the extra cash and give it to my mother to pay off "our debt." For years I was disappointed with Mrs. G. for what I believed she had done to my mother. On one occasion I visited her in the hospital and had planned to get it off my chest, after all those years. However, she was too ill for me to bring it up. In fact, I never discussed it with either her or my mother. Years later I wondered whether I should have discussed it the weekend that I found out mom was working. The truth is that I assumed and really don't know how things unfolded. I watched and learned that my mother had a lot of pride, so it would not have been out of the ordinary for her to have decided to do extra work in order to tell herself that she had not accepted a "handout" but paid for her son's first year in college herself! So, the idea of working some evenings and weekends may very well have been my mother's idea. I will never know what happened, but will always be grateful that Mrs. G. "stepped up to the plate" and changed my whole life and career trajectory!

Mrs. G. had two daughters. We did not have very much interaction when we were growing up. I would see them from time to time, but that was it. They loved my mother and she loved them. At times she talked about them as though they were her daughters. I suppose that is how many housekeepers felt about the children they helped to raise. My mother eventually took another job. I convinced her that she needed to find employment where there were health and retirement benefits. She did not want to leave them, but she understood my concern for her well-being. One of her friends attempted to get her to sue the family for paying her in cash each week and not providing any fringe benefits. This family friend might as well have been talking to our cat because there was no likelihood that my mother would ever have considered such a thing. She really loved the family! During the year 2016, I was reading an email and much to my surprise, one of the many recipients of the email had the same name as one of Mrs. G.'s daughters. I was going to ignore it, but my curiosity would not allow it. Could this be the daughter of Mrs. G. from Connecticut?

I was so curious about this possibility that I sent an email asking if she grew up in Connecticut. I indicated that I was Dora's son. She responded by asking if I was James Earl, a name only used by my family members. We confirmed that we knew each other even though it had been many years since we last talked. She sent me a photo of us at her wedding reception in 1980 and expressed how happy she was that we brought my mother to be with her on such a special day. In November of 2019 she surprised me with an email indicating that she was traveling with a group that was going on a trip through the South. They had just completed a course called "Jews and the Modern Civil Rights Movement" and wanted to visit some of the places they had studied. She indicated that they were going to stop in Atlanta and wondered if my wife and I had time to meet her for dinner. I met her for dinner and had a good time reminiscing. Back at the hotel she introduced me to a couple of her traveling companions. One of them was quite curious about our meeting each other after nearly forty years. To be honest I wasn't sure what she would say. Would she tell them that my mother used to be their maid or housekeeper? After discussing my first presidency she simply said that we were former high school friends. It was obvious that her friend still wanted to know the "real story." On my ride home that evening, I really understood what the producers of the 2011 film *The Help* were trying to communicate. Having dinner with Mrs. G.'s daughter and discussing our lives growing up was like having a conversation with a relative that I had not seen in a long time.

Back to my first days on campus. I had already checked, and we had a laundry room in the building, so I could wash my clothes, dry them, iron them, and put them on the next day. Word soon spread around the campus that there was a "colored" kid in Tolland Hall who was so poor that he had to wash his clothes every night so that he could wear them the next day. Even I heard about the "colored" kid who was standing in the laundry room naked because all his clothes were in the dryer. I never stood there naked, but that is what circulated around the campus. Soon students from other dormitories were walking past our laundry to get a glimpse of "the naked colored kid." This craziness only lasted a few days because my mother brought me some jeans and khakis that weekend. Now I had five pairs of pants and several sweatshirts, so I was good to go. I no longer had to wash clothes every night.

I had some very interesting roommates during my first two years at UConn. The first one was very nice. He did not seem to care that his roommate was Black, although he admitted that he had not been around enough Black people to have formed an opinion about us. When his parents were preparing to leave our room, they said, "Goodbye, be sure to keep an eye on our son for us." Little did I know that they were serious. He had some hygiene issues that got him in trouble with the resident advisors. One Friday afternoon his parents came to pick him up to take him home for the weekend, or so everyone thought. I knew that it was not the case because he took all his personal belongings with him. For whatever reason, they decided to withdraw him from the university. My second roommate was the son of two corporate executives. His parents provided him with all the finer things in life. He went to the best schools, wore the latest fashions, and drove a very nice convertible sports car. He had it all. When he entered the room and saw me sitting behind the desk, I could tell that we had a problem. The fact that I was a poor kid from the projects made things even worse.

If ever there was an example of privilege, he was it. Having attended a very prestigious boarding school, he was not supposed to be at UConn. He should have been at an Ivy League college or at least an elite private college. So, he arrived at UConn with a chip on his shoulder because he was better than the rest of us, Black or white. So how could he ever accept being at a state land-grant university that was founded "for the sons and daughters of the working class"?

Every time we talked about race, economics, social mobility, and the value of a college degree, it became a shouting match. One evening we had a fight because he called me the "n word." We could not have been any more different if the computer had been programmed to put two opposites together. To make matters even more complicated, he was an agnostic, and I was Pentecostal. He questioned why I would be content to graduate from college and take a job as a teacher. For him, that was no money. He pointed out that he would not have been in college if that was all he could accomplish. His goal was to make a six-figure salary, then who knows what. It was very difficult for him to understand that I didn't know five people in the world making the money he was talking about. Even our professors weren't making the kind of salary that he considered the lowest he would work for. The students directly across the hall from us were white guys who grew up on a farm. One night he told them that he had more in common with me than he had with them; "at least we both bought our milk from the grocery store." Once we both stopped trying to convert the other one and began to listen to what was being said, things got much better. We both acknowledged that having been placed in the room together gave us an education we never expected. When my sons began discussing college attendance, there was one item that was nonnegotiable. I insisted that they spend the first semester in a college residence hall because the education they would get there was, in some ways, as valuable as that which they would receive in the classroom.

Studying at UConn during the early 1960s was a real challenge for African American students. I heard that there were twelve of us on campus my freshman year. While I don't know if that was true, I do know that when we walked past each other, there was an unspoken acknowledgement that this was really tough. But I had something that a few others may not have had. Being part of the track team gave me a group of students and staff with whom I could bond. I had a support system. The first time I went to speak with the head coach about my desire to join the track team, he humiliated me when I told him that I was a pole vaulter. He laughed and said, "You don't look big enough or fast enough to be a college pole vaulter." I reminded him of that when I set a school record! Coach Duff and Assistant Coach Kennedy became strong supporters of mine and served as a character reference for me for many years. In his reference letters Coach Duff always spoke about our first meeting and the fact that I did not let his comments shape who I would become on the track.

I also had a support system in the Spanish Department. The faculty, especially a visiting scholar from Spain, Dr. Gabriel Rosado, seemed fascinated by my interest in Spanish language and literature. I guess it seemed unusual to them that a student from public housing in New Haven could become so interested in the University of Salamanca, an institution founded in 1218, and in Miguel de Cervantes's work *Don Quixote de la Mancha*. So, when I wasn't at track practice, I was in the Foreign Language Department. There was also a music professor with whom I connected. He later commented that I entered his class bragging about the Platters, and Frankie Lymon and the Teenagers, but left his course with a love for Maurice Ravel's *Boléro*! Several years later as a graduate student, I would study the issue of student retention. Student retention rates were high among students who established a personal relationship with a faculty or staff member. I am sure that the close relationships I had with faculty helped me survive some of the difficult days at the university.

Struggling to adjust and adapt to a very new and different campus environment was only half the battle. I would soon learn that going back home wouldn't be so easy. Some of my friends were not happy that I left the "hood" and went to college. During my first semester I decided not to return home until the Thanksgiving break so that people would really miss me. I purchased a UConn sweatshirt to wear to the Thanksgiving Day high school football game hoping that all my friends would notice it and ask me about college. That is exactly what happened. The game went well, I spoke to a lot of my friends, and then headed home. My mother asked me to bring in my clothes, which she had washed and hung out on the line to dry. I informed her that there were no clothes on the line. When she went outside and saw that there were no clothes on the line, she figured that someone had taken down the wrong clothes by mistake. However, no one returned the clothes Thursday, Friday, or Saturday. Fortunately, I had not brought all of my clothes home to be washed or I would have had to go back to campus with nothing. On another trip home with a few college friends, we decided to attend a Yale University football game. When my friends ordered hot dogs and Cokes just before halftime, the young man who sold them to us turned to me and said, "What are you looking at, Lyons, you were out here with us last year selling hotdogs." The only thing I could say at that point was, "You are right, and I saved all of the money I made in order to go to college. I still have dollar bills with mustard on them!" Everybody laughed, including the young man who was trying to embarrass me in front of my college friends.

More than twenty years later, while taking my sons on "an education trip" back to the neighborhood where I grew up, I learned that my friends had deliberately taken my clothes off of the clothesline that Thanksgiving weekend because they did not want me to return to college. They reasoned that if I didn't have any clothes I would not return to campus. They were afraid that I would forget them or, worse, turn my back on them! There was nothing that I did to suggest that I felt I was better than them, which they admitted. But it was the fear that with a college education, Jimmy would think that he was superior to the guys with whom he had spent most of his life. There was a challenge for me both on and off campus. But that was a learning experience because it taught me that for the rest of my life, I would have to learn to operate in two worlds, the academy and the hood!

My first job after college was in New Bedford, Massachusetts, at the Fort Rodman Job Corps Center. The Job Corps was founded in 1964 by Sargent Shriver to offer free education and vocational training to young men and women ages sixteen to twenty-four. I enjoyed working at the Job Corps. A number of the staff members had served in the Peace Corps, and after two years of listening to their stories, I decided to apply. The Peace Corps was a tremendous experience because it gave me the opportunity to live and travel abroad. After the Peace Corps, I landed in Philadelphia where I taught Spanish at Wagner Junior High School. Imagine trying to convince students from North Philadelphia, in 1967, that it was important to study a foreign language. A few of them liked the idea, but most of them saw no relevance at all. I enjoyed teaching in the public schools of Philadelphia and probably would have remained there for more than two years had I not received a call from the University of Connecticut.

I was really enjoying living and working in Philadelphia. I got married in 1967 to the girl that I met on the way to see Senator John F.

Kennedy; I was enjoying teaching Spanish to junior high school students, and I was enjoying my part-time work at Temple University. At that time, there were probably more former Peace Corps volunteers in this "City of Brotherly Love" than in any city in America. School Superintendent Mark Shed believed that Peace Corps Volunteers had the kind of "stuff" that was special, and he wanted us in Philadelphia working for the school district. It was during the spring of 1969 that I received a phone call from a former UConn classmate Bill Trueheart, who was working as an intern on the campus. He indicated that the university was looking for a director of the Afro-American Cultural Center and had been unsuccessful in the search. They were having difficulty finding a candidate that was acceptable to both the students and to the administration. He felt that I would be a good candidate for the position because I was from New Haven and could relate to the inner city African American students. I had lived in Latin America and had trained for the Peace Corps in Puerto Rico, so the Puerto Rican students might find that attractive. The position was very interesting in that the director was a member of the student personnel staff, was an advisor to the African American students, and would be responsible for bringing the African American cultural experience to the campus. After speaking with my wife, I decided to go for the interview.

The interview went well. The student affairs staff had done their homework and it was obvious that they had talked to a number of people who knew me from my undergraduate student years, as well as my involvement with the track team, the Spanish club, and the yearbook. To be honest, the only thing about the interview that I didn't like was the fact that the students referred to the Afro-American Cultural Center as the "Black House." I knew why they called it that and just accepted the fact that if I took the position, people of all ethnic groups would have to get used to coming to my office in the "Black House." Upon my return home I had a lot to discuss with my wife. After thinking about it and praying about it, we decided to make the move. I called Bill and told him I would accept the job. This time when I traveled to Storrs, I had more than just the clothes on my back. But interestingly enough, our apartment, the Northwood Apartments, was on the same road, North Eagleville Road, that I lived on as a freshman.

The position was all that I dreamed of and more. A quick survey around the country revealed that I may have been the only one in the country with such a position. In other words, there were African American personnel doing one position or the other, but the combination of responsibilities and reporting lines made my position unique. The late sixties were difficult days for college campuses given all the student activism. We didn't know from one day to the next what was going to happen. The most exciting part of the job was bringing Black entertainment to the campus. While it was clear to everyone that I was bringing people to campus for the Black students, I also wanted to introduce the university community to the Black experience. I worked closely with the staff, who oversaw the university auditorium, and had experience bringing performing artists to the campus. When I brought the poet Nikki Giovanni, the audience was nearly all Black and young. On the other hand, when I invited pianist Andre Watts to perform, some Black students complained that they could not get tickets because "the white folks had bought them all." On one occasion I invited a young man from New York City to speak. I had not heard him speak, but the students strongly recommended him to me. Years later, in 1992, at a funeral on the campus of Jackson State University, I would ask minister Louis Farrakhan if he remembered being invited to the University of Connecticut back in the early seventies, and he said yes. I informed him that I was who brought him there.

During my time in this position, I brought a lot of celebrities and entertainers to the campus. The guest who brought the greatest amount of attention was Muhammad Ali. I scheduled him to come to campus to speak to the university community. This announcement created a lot of excitement on campus because on June 28, 1971, the United States Supreme Court decided the case of *Clay v. United States*. It overturned his conviction for failure to enter the military. This meant that our campus would be one of the first large gatherings at which he would speak following the court's decision. Not only was the campus excited, but we were too. His agent had indicated that Ali would arrive in town early, so we knew we would have to entertain him. How do you entertain the heavyweight champion of the world in the Northwood Apartments? My wife was very concerned about what to serve him because he didn't eat pork, and we had no idea if he had any dietary restrictions due to his training schedule.

Early that afternoon we received a phone call from Ali indicating that he was in town in front of a restaurant. I told him that I would come and meet him, and I would be driving a Ford Mustang. When I asked how I would recognize him, he answered, "I am probably the only person in the area driving a Rolls Royce!" At that point Jocelyn and I knew we were in for a long afternoon. When he arrived at the apartment, he and his wife Belinda made themselves at home. We were very concerned about what to serve him for lunch, which he soon solved for us by going into our refrigerator and asking, "What's this?" We informed him that it was leftover roast beef, and he said fine, "That's what we will eat." While the ladies prepared our late lunch, Ali wanted to go outside in the yard. When the neighborhood children saw him, they ran over to him to take photos. He "shadow boxed" with them and really put on a show. Before long the word spread that Muhammad Ali was at the Northwood Apartments. So many people made their way to the apartments that we needed the campus police to help out. Back inside the apartment, he asked to hold our oldest son who was just a baby. When he handed Jimmy back to me, we all noticed a wet spot on his clothes. Our son had wet on the heavyweight champion of the world!

I really enjoyed bringing well-known individuals to the campus to expose both the Black students and the broader community to the Black experience. We all received an education that might not have taken place were it not for the Center. I attempted to bring people to the campus who would not offend other groups as they shared their expertise. At the same time, I wanted them to be honest and speak their minds. On the personal level I often had to "pinch myself" to make certain that this was really happening. Did this young man from Dixwell Avenue really spend the afternoon with Muhammad Ali? When Nina Simone sat in my office talking with a small group of students and staff, I asked myself if this was my purpose. Was I put on this planet to make these kinds of dialogues happen?

My experience in Ecuador in the Peace Corps proved to be quite valuable in a way that I had not expected. When I started talking with universities about a PhD program, it became obvious that there were some universities that might admit me based on my international experience, and their personal interest in having a graduate student in the department who had firsthand experience working in a developing country. In a couple of instances, it felt quite good to have a suitor. But whatever decision I made had to be made based on what was best for my family and me. I can admit that my heart was still in Latin America. I took advantage of every opportunity to further this interest by attending activities and programs at UConn that were focused on Latin America. The university was gaining a reputation for its strength in Latin American Studies, and several of the academic departments could benefit from having a graduate student on board with my experience. However, the fact that I was already doing graduate work in the UConn School of Education, and the fact that the campus turbulence of the times cried out for more people to be trained in higher education administration, made it quite easy for me to decide to remain in the School of Education and pursue the terminal degree. I would still be able to interact with the Latin American scholars on the campus.

Dr. Floyd Bass, the director of Black studies and professor of education, was very interested in and concerned about the young African American professionals whom the university had started hiring. He told me that I should plan to go to graduate school if I wanted to work in higher education. He wanted to make it clear that we should not become so enamored with our current positions that we lose our real focus, which should be on the future. When I accepted the position of director of the Afro-American Cultural Center, I had not planned to apply to graduate school, but after some time on the campus, I knew it was the right thing to do. I was working in the student-personnel division, so it made sense for me to enroll in the master's degree program in student personnel. Taking these courses not only gave me the formal credentials for this type of work, but it introduced me to faculty and staff in the School of Education. Even before I had completed this program Dr. Bass was suggesting that I pursue the doctorate. Again, I listened to the man who would later become my major advisor in my PhD program in higher education administration.

I discussed the idea of a PhD program with my wife, and she was very supportive. In fact, she decided to apply to the master's degree program in elementary education because she had done some teaching in Philadelphia and enjoyed working with young children. The word circulated among Black graduate students on campus that the graduate admissions office in the School of Education really gave Black applicants a difficult time at the interview. Before my interview, I was personally advised not to get angry, act professionally, and after some criticism I would probably be admitted. I was scheduled to be interviewed at 1:00 p.m. and my wife at 3:00 p.m. I will always be grateful for the "heads up" that I received from Black doctoral students in the School of Education. If they had not advised me to be calm and be patient, I may have said something that would have ruined my chances of being admitted. First, during the interview I was informed that my GRE score was not good, and that the School of Education had to "maintain some standards," even though it was committed to bringing in more Black graduate students.

Next it was pointed out that I had been a weak student at the undergraduate level and was lucky to have graduated. However, my performance in the master's program was very good and, in his opinion, compensated for my weak undergraduate record. I really did not understand why my undergraduate record was relevant given that I had finished the master's program! But I continued to be patient waiting for him to say that I was admitted. He finally mentioned my score on the Miller Analogies Test (MAT). He couldn't understand how one could do so poorly on the GRE but be in the top 1 percent on the MAT. He asked if I realized that my MAT score was better than most of the other students applying to graduate school? I answered "yes." It didn't take much imagination for me to read between the lines and understand that I was being told that my MAT score was better than 99 percent of the white applicants. He finally said, "We are admitting you into the doctoral program" and stood up and extended his hand. I thanked him and left his office immediately. I then went to find my wife, and when I found her, I let her know that what we had heard was true, and she should sit there and grit her teeth if she had to, but he would admit her into the program.

In addition to a good job, and the opportunity to return to Storrs, Connecticut, we were blessed by the birth of our first two sons. Our oldest son James (whom we call Jimmy) and middle son Jamal were both born while we were graduate students at the University of Connecticut. The youngest son, Jack, was born in Delaware eight years later. Working a full-time job during the day, going to graduate school at night, and trying to raise a family was not easy. But we did, as a couple, what was required to succeed. I worked very hard in graduate school and felt privileged to have several people in the graduate School of Education express a genuine interest in my success as a graduate student and as a young professional. I can remember nights that my wife and I sat at the table doing our schoolwork, while passing the baby back and forth. During one semester our classes were back-to-back. She arrived early for her class and brought our son with her. She would stand outside and wait for my class to end so that I could watch the baby. If my professor talked too long, she would be late for her class. One evening Dr. Mark Shibles saw her in the hall with the baby and announced to our class, "I guess it's time for me to shut up and end this class." But the important thing was that even though there were some challenges, I completed the program and celebrated the moment with my wife, who completed her master's degree that same semester, and faculty and staff in the higher education administration program. On the day of graduation, I stood there taking photos with my doctoral regalia on. I was so proud of my doctoral robe and my hood displaying the colors signifying the discipline of education. It was 1973, and I was leaving UConn quite differently than I had arrived in 1961, twelve years earlier. This time I was fully clothed in the trappings of academia!

Chapter 4

# SERENDIPITY

*Merriam-Webster* defines "serendipity" as "the gift of finding valuable or agreeable things not sought for." *The Webster's New World College Dictionary* defines it as "luck or good fortune, in finding something good accidentally." Finally, a colleague of mine, who writes a lot about spirituality, refers to it as "fate, or the finger of God." Each of these definitions suggest that there are times when things happened that you were not seeking, nor expecting, but you benefitted from them. Or, you ask yourself how things might have been different were it not for this surprise event or result. I have written this chapter because a lot of things happened during my career that were not expected or sought after. In each case there remains the question what might have happened if this had not occurred at the time? Would I have gone forward on a different journey? Would I be writing these words from a different perspective? Would my life have been totally different?

The very first event I would mention here is one that I have discussed earlier, about my going to college as a result of my mother's boss. As I stated earlier, the reason that Mrs. G. and my mother had a conversation at all was because her sister was sick and she agreed to take her niece to college. She knew that my mom did not have a car, so she was willing to take me. That led to the conversation and the revelation that I was not going because we did not have the money. I have often thought about what might have happened if her sister had not been sick and drove her own daughter off to college as most parents do. Would there have been any discussion about my college plans? Is it possible that I would never have made it to college? One person's illness, who was in no way directly connected to me, turned my life in a different direction. Instead of retiring from higher education having served in six college and university presidencies, would I have retired from the Air Force as a major or a lieutenant colonel?

I guess I will never know because things worked out well. One of the important takeaways here is that I had worked hard in high school and had been admitted to college. I simply did not have the money to attend. I still encounter young people in that same situation today and feel quite comfortable making suggestions to them and their parents about how they should prepare for college financially.

A second event happened following my junior year in college, and it too involved the military. The University of Connecticut is a land-grant university, and as a result of the Land Grant Act, ROTC had to be offered for the first two years. I selected the Air Force ROTC program rather than the Army ROTC program. Unlike many of my classmates, I really enjoyed it and started to ask myself if I should pursue a career in the military, as I had considered when I was about to finish high school. This time, I would enter the Air Force as a second lieutenant. For two years I worked very hard to be the best that I could be, and it was paying off. I spit shined my shoes and my hat brim so the officers would know that I was a serious cadet. Those who showed the promise that I did were encouraged to take the physical and then go to advanced camp. I could not wait to go to Fort Devens, Massachusetts, and take my physical. This would be the start of an exciting new life for me; first as a student in the advanced ROTC program, and after graduation, a pilot in the United States Air Force. Well, before I could leave the fort, I was told that the doctors who examined me had determined that I was color blind and had a heart murmur, both of which disqualified me from the advanced ROTC program. I knew that I had a functional heart murmur, but I had been cleared to run track by a Yale University cardiologist, so I believed that I was okay. If my heart was a problem, how could I have been cleared to run track each year? This was now the second time that I had considered the military as a career option. The first time I said no thanks; this time they said no thanks. If I had been by myself, I probably would have cried all the way back to campus because I was really crushed. However, on a bus full of young men, I was not going to shed one tear. This incident left emotional scars, but the next one left physical scars.

During the summer following my junior year at UConn, just a few months following my disappointing trip to Fort Devens, I took a construction job. I had begun to enjoy a measure of success as a university pole vaulter. Competitors from other universities knew that when they came to UConn, they would have to bring their A game in order to beat me. Although I was small in stature compared to most vaulters, I did well because I mastered the technique. A construction job would give me an opportunity to grow stronger and build my muscles. I was grateful to the track coach for finally awarding me a scholarship that would cover most of my senior-year expenses. I owed it to him to return to school in good condition and stronger than I had been the past three years. There was already talk about the 1968 Summer Olympic Games in Mexico City, and I dreamed about doing well enough to compete in the Olympic trials. After only a few weeks on the construction job I was the victim of an accident. It was my responsibility to signal to the crane operator to move the shovel; but someone else did it, and I was snatched up in the air. My screams caught the attention of the crane operator, and he lowered the shovel.

I was taken to a nearby hospital and rushed into surgery. I remember lying on the table and hearing the doctor say, "Let's see if we can save some of these fingers." I have long claimed that I probably didn't need any anesthesia because when I heard what the doctor said I am sure that I fainted! After a few hours of surgery, I was taken to a room where I remained for several days. My right hand was crushed, but the doctor whose voice I had heard was a top orthopedic surgeon, who just happened to work in this comparatively small hospital in Meriden, Connecticut. The nurses told me that I was very fortunate to have had this surgeon because there were others who probably would have chosen to amputate some or all of the fingers on my right hand. The owner of the construction company claimed that it was a routine work-related accident and that I would be covered by his insurance. I did not believe that it was that simple, because his sixteen-year-old nephew was on site that day and I heard him giving instructions to some of the workers. But that was the official position, and I couldn't prove otherwise. Years later I heard that the owner's nephew gave the crane operator the signal to pull the shovel up out of the hole, instead of allowing me to do it. I also heard that all the workers who saw what happened were given new cars as a bribe, to keep their mouths shut. It was clear to me that I would not be pole vaulting any time soon, if ever, but that was okay; I was more concerned about being able to use my hand than I was pole vaulting at the Olympic trials.

When I returned to campus, everyone was shocked to see my arm in a sling and my right hand completely bandaged. I had to tell the story about the summer construction job accident more times than can be imagined. The track coaches were sympathetic and told me not to worry about anything. I really appreciated that because this was my first time on a full athletic scholarship and I would not be able to vault. When my arm was taken out of the sling, I decided that I would begin hanging out with the track team again. Soon I had an idea that I discussed privately with the athletic trainer hoping to get his agreement before doing anything. I indicated that I wanted to participate in an event that was new to me but was gaining popularity in New England colleges and universities. It was the hop, step, and jump, more commonly called the triple jump. I wanted to know if the trainer could tape my hand in a way that would allow me to fall to the ground without doing further damage to my fingers. I went out to the track a couple of times after everyone had left to see if my plan would work. As I landed in the pit it became obvious that I would have to fall on my side in order to avoid landing on my hand, even with it taped. This would not be the best form and might cause me to lose a few inches in distance, but it would allow me to compete. I also discussed this matter with the insurance company just to make sure that I would not jeopardize my workman's compensation. They said that it was okay because I was not pole vaulting.

You can imagine the shock on the coach's face when I told him that I was returning to the team and wanted to compete in the triple jump! He knew that I had never done it before, but rather than discourage me he remembered that as a freshman he had told me that I didn't "look like a pole vaulter." It was not an easy decision because I would have to remove the sling from my arm and lose all the attention and benefits that came with it like others taking notes for me, carrying my tray in the cafeteria, and carrying my books when I needed the help. But it was the right decision. I worked very hard trying to master the technique of the triple jump. It wasn't long before I was doing well enough to score points in most of our meets. My landing style was a bit awkward, but the coach didn't care because I was scoring points for the team. I never pole vaulted again, and I believe the insurance company sent a man to our track meets to spy on me and make certain that I was not collecting a check under false pretenses. Several of us noticed a man who would show up at every home track meet and watch what was going on in the pole vault and the triple jump. At one point one of the trainers asked him if he had a child or other relative on the team and he responded that he just liked to watch the team. I regret that the injury ended my career as a pole vaulter, but it gave me the opportunity to try another event that proved to be very positive for me personally and for the team. Some of my church members used my experience to support one of their favorite sayings: "When one door closes, God will open another one."

Another event that happened serendipitously took place during my senior year in college. I decided that I would talk with Dr. Rosado about pursuing a graduate degree in Spanish language and literature at the University of Madrid. As a Spanish major I had studied a lot of literature and found it enjoyable. Perhaps I was really preparing myself for a career as a professor of Spanish. During the early spring of my senior year, I applied and was admitted to the University of Madrid in Spain. I sent money to reserve space in a boarding house not too far from the campus. I had no money to fly to Madrid, so I reserved space on a cruise ship going from New York to Madrid. They agreed to let me work on the ship to cover my travel expenses. Everything seemed to have fallen in place. I was all set to go, and started telling people that I was going to Spain following graduation. Here I come, Madrid!

As we got closer to commencement, many of my friends were still interviewing and applying for jobs. On the day that I was going to pick up my tuxedo for the senior prom, a friend asked me to pick his up and drop it off at the placement office. He had an interview with a new organization called the Job Corps and did not want to miss it. I said okay. The gentleman who was doing the recruiting invited me to come in, but I told him no thanks. I explained that I was going to the University of Madrid and was not looking for a job; I was okay waiting in the hallway. The truth was that I could hear everything he was saying. He explained that all of the corpsmen were high school dropouts, many of whom came from Los Angeles. Some had been involved in the Watts Riot and were given the choice of going to jail for arson and looting or entering the Job Corps. I was so impressed with the idea of the Job Corps that I called the recruiter, and he accepted my application with open arms. I started my first job out of college in late September of 1965 in New Bedford, Massachusetts, at the Fort Rodman Job Corps. The "interview" that I overheard from the hallway was very much unexpected. I had no intention whatsoever of changing my plan to attend graduate school at the University of Madrid. Years later I asked myself what would have happened to me career-wise if I had told Lou that I would take his tuxedo back to the dormitory instead of the placement office? Would I still have gone to Spain? I think so. More than fifty years later Lou and I discussed this turn of events. He laughed about the fact that he decided not to go to work for the Job Corps and instead go to graduate school.

Everyone was shocked to hear that I would not be going to Spain but instead would stay in the US to help further this new and exciting program. One of my Spanish professors told me that my decision made him conclude that my life and career would be one of service, even if it meant personal sacrifice. I think he was right! The idea of helping these young boys "get on the right track" was more important to me at that time than going to graduate school. Do I ever wonder what might have happened if I had gone on to Spain? Yes, I do. Had I gone on to graduate school at the University of Madrid, I would have been on a track to become a full-time college professor. But I made the choice to go in a different direction at that time, and I have no regrets.

The next serendipitous incident occurred when I was the vice president for academic affairs at Delaware State University, in Dover, Delaware. Things were going well, and I was thinking about remaining at Delaware State until the president retired and then applying for the position. When I was hired the board members had let it be known that they really wanted someone who might be ready to assume the presidency when Dr. Mishoe retired. We had our third son Jack while living in Delaware, and the older two seemed to be growing up fast. I had been there four years and honestly felt that I could do another four years easily. I enjoyed working with President Mishoe and was able to sit with him and "pick his brain" on key higher education issues. He had been there many years and enjoyed sharing his wisdom with me. As a result, there was no pressure on me to start applying for college presidencies. This I explained to several search firms that called me when they were conducting presidential searches.

One morning I received a call from the American Council on Education (ACE) asking if I would be free later that week to interview candidates for the ACE Fellows Program. The person that was scheduled to do it got sick, and they were looking for someone close by who could drive over to DC and spend a day. I was free on the day in question and could easily do a two-and-a-half-hour drive to One Dupont Circle. They overnighted some material for me to review, and I was good to go. When I arrived at the ACE office, we were divided up in teams of two and the schedule was developed in a way that would allow each team to interview all the candidates by the end of the day. I was paired up with a woman from Annapolis, Maryland, who worked for the state college and university system. Just before we broke for lunch my interview partner made a more formal introduction of herself than she had made in the group setting. She indicated that she was very impressed with me based on how I engaged the candidates and wondered if I had an interest in a presidency they were trying to fill. When she identified Bowie State College as the campus, I told her that I had received a call from the search firm but had no interest in leaving Delaware. During a midafternoon break, she advised me that "today is the last day for applications and nominations, and if you can get someone to fax a nomination letter to our office you would meet the deadline for candidates." After being asked a third time and having her point out that it would not hurt to apply even if I was happy at Delaware State, I finally said that I would.

I agreed to ask the president of the American Council on Education for a nomination letter, which went in before the 5:00 p.m. deadline. After asking me to apply, she made it very clear that she was not promising me the job and acknowledged that she had no official role in the process. The president was hired by their board of trustees. All she was trying to do was to help identify potential applicants. I was later contacted by the search firm indicating that I was among a group of applicants who had passed the first round of screening. When I was later notified that I had made the short list of candidates and was being invited to a hotel near the Baltimore-Washington International Airport for an interview, I was pleasantly surprised. A short time after the off-campus interview, I was notified that the board was prepared to offer me the position of president of Bowie State College. I accepted the position and started my first college presidency, in July of 1983, at the age of thirty-nine. Once again, because someone became sick, an opportunity was laid before me that I pursued. I am also aware of the fact that I had made a favorable impression on a perfect stranger because of the way I spoke, asked questions, and conducted myself with the applicants. She could see that I had considerable knowledge about American higher education. Of course, I have wondered how things might have developed career-wise if I had not chosen to interview ACE Fellows that week. I have no idea how long I would have remained at Delaware State waiting for the president to retire. The facts were clear: I was offered the position and made the decision to "take the bird in the hand" and move to Maryland. Bowie State was my home for the next nine years, my longest presidency.

Another serendipitous story is based completely on rumors, but given that I heard it from some very reliable sources I will discuss it here. I agreed to submit my credentials for the presidency of California State University, Dominguez Hills. When the chancellor of the California State University system heard this, he arranged for us to meet at the Dulles International Airport in Washington, DC. Both of us had return flights later that afternoon but had allowed sufficient time for a lengthy conversation should that be necessary. After some general comments about Southern California and the Los Angeles area in particular, the chancellor told me about the need for someone with considerable higher education experience who could appreciate making a contribution at the most racially and ethnically diverse university in the system and perhaps in the state. He was also aware that I had been a finalist for the presidency at Cal State Hayward, another institution in the system, a few years earlier. The most important point that he wanted to leave with me was the fact that the university had been placed on "warning" by its regional accreditor, and the next president would have to work hard to resolve the accreditation issues. We agreed that I would become a serious candidate and would meet at some point in the future with the system's board of trustees.

My subsequent meeting with the board of trustees went very well. As a result, I was offered the position. After arriving on campus, I went to work immediately rallying the campus stakeholders around our efforts. Everyone pitched in and did what was necessary to get the job done. As a result, our regional accreditation agency, WASC, removed us from warning. One evening, as we celebrated our success, I was approached by a Latino staff member and a Latino student. They expressed that while they were very pleased with what I had accomplished, they were disappointed that Dominguez Hills did not hire its first Latino president. They believed that if the faculty had not "messed up" the institutional self-study, the campus would not have been placed on warning. Therefore, the Latino person who was rumored to already have been identified would have been offered the job. I wasn't sure what to think about this revelation until I heard it again from a senior member of the faculty. What he said was that the faculty had been so frustrated with the previous administration that they "cried out for help" from the visiting accreditation team. This strategy backfired, and the university was placed on warning. So as a result, my strong background of working with regional accreditation agencies moved my application "to the top of the pile." Whether it was true or not, a lot of people on the campus believed that I would not have been offered the position at Dominguez Hills if the faculty had not "screwed up" the campus visit! What a welcoming.

The final story is as much a lesson learned as it was serendipity. By the spring of 1992 I knew that in all likelihood I was going to be a Tiger in the fall, either a Tennessee State University Tiger or a Jackson State University Tiger. When the firms conducting the respective searches informed me that I had made the short list for a campus interview, I had to decide which of these two well-known institutions would be the best fit. I knew very little about Jackson State. Every time I mentioned Jackson State to someone, they indicated that it was Walter Payton's alma mater. There was a former graduate school classmate of mine on the faculty, but we had not seen each other or had a conversation in years. I knew only a little bit more about Tennessee State because I visited the campus while writing my dissertation. I was invited to both campuses for an interview and understood that I was going to have to decide how to proceed. Even though both searches were supposed to be confidential, in terms of the names of the finalists, given the higher education communications network or the "grapevine," as I used to call it, search committee members would find out that I was a finalist at another university. I did my homework and went to each interview very well prepared. I had a good story to tell about my experience at Bowie, so I considered it to be my strongest asset.

The real challenge that I faced at both institutions was that I had not attended a historically Black institution. I could produce solid evidence and results from my work at five such institutions, but there was always someone on the search committee who would eliminate me as a candidate because I attended a "white" school and couldn't possibly understand the culture of an HBCU. I anticipated this discussion at both interviews and would deal with it at that time. Both campus visits went well. Rumor had it that I was the first choice of both search committees, but I understood the reality that the governing boards and not the search committees would select the president. After doing a little more "research" I learned the name of the other finalist for the Tennessee State position. I decided to withdraw from the Tennessee search all but assuring that he would get the position as the sole finalist. I began to focus all my attention on Jackson State. I was very pleased with my reception on campus and felt that if people could get over my being a Yankee, things would work out in my favor. A couple of years later I learned that while I might have been the first choice of the Jackson State search committee, I was the second choice of the commissioner. His first choice was a candidate who lived in Georgia, and if that candidate's wife had agreed to join him in Jackson, he would have accepted the position. So, my decision to withdraw from the Tennessee State search almost cost me both jobs. I guess I should thank the other candidate's wife. Would I have been able to convince the board in Maryland to let me remain at Bowie even though they knew that I was pursuing two other positions? I guess I will never know. Lesson learned!

# Chapter 5

# FROM THE JOB CORPS
# TO THE PEACE CORPS

The Peace Corps experience may not have been directly related to my journey from the projects to the presidency, but there were many lessons learned from that experience that would help shape my philosophy about life. While I had always wanted to travel, my initial concern was that the Peace Corps might send me to a place where I did not want to be, doing something that I did not want to do. After much encouragement, and some prodding, I made the decision to apply. My decision to leave the Job Corps was not made frivolously, because one of the most important lessons that I have learned throughout my working career took place while I was at the Job Corps. There was a young man in my dormitory whom I enjoyed working with and getting to know. I saw potential in him and made a personal commitment to do all that I could to help him be a success.

He grew up in a major urban area and soon decided that school was not for him; so, he dropped out. He considered himself to be a "hustler" and was doing some things that were illegal. I never really knew what the motivating factor was, but he decided to enter the Job Corps. This would get him off the street for a while, and he could complete his GED and get a job. I enjoyed listening to him and at times counseled him as though he were my son. I spent a lot of time with him; in fact, there were days when I spent more time with him than all the other corpsmen combined. I was convinced that he could complete the program and return home with a good job. One afternoon a detective came to our center looking for him. I was shocked. As it turned out he had done something illegal and would be forced to leave the Job Corps. I accompanied him to Logan Airport in Boston and at that time was able to walk with him to the gate. As we stood at the gate, he told me something that I would remember for the rest of my life. He thanked me for all the time that I had spent with him trying to help him turn his life around, but he wanted me to understand that "I did not want what you wanted for me! I am okay going back out on the street 'hustling,' but I will be okay." As I left the airport and started the drive back to New Bedford, I was so full of sadness that I began to question my fitness for this type of work. I thought about the many young men in the dormitory who really wanted to turn their lives around and just needed support and a little encouragement; yet I spent much of my time with someone who didn't want to change. This incident hurt me badly, but I learned a lesson early in my education and teaching career. You cannot save everyone, no matter how hard you try! From that moment on I decided that I would "go the last mile" trying to help children and students, but they had to show me that they really wanted it. As the saying goes, they would have to have some skin in the game.

I made it through the Peace Corps application process quite easily, but remained uncomfortable about where I might be assigned. The Peace Corps was recruiting in Boston for a couple of days, so I decided to go and meet with someone face to face and talk about the process. He told me that I could not pick both the country and the program. If my priority was to serve in a Spanish-speaking country, that was okay, but the Peace Corps would decide which program I would join. So, I decided to take that approach and make myself available to serve in any program of their choosing, as long as it was in a Spanish-speaking country. I was admitted to the Peace Corps in 1966 and told that I would be going to Ecuador to be part of a physical education/coaching program. They were excited by my background in track and field, and the Spanish language ability I had developed in college. Our group was going to Denison University in Granville, Ohio, for our initial training, and then on to San Juan, Puerto Rico, for the final phase of the training. Denison was a twenty-five-minute drive from Columbus, but it was made very clear that we would not have much time to visit. We spent all day in class where we were given instruction on how to teach physical education, and how to coach basketball and track. With the Mexico City Summer Olympics just two years away, some of us might be coaching Olympic hopefuls. As a standard part of our training, we had to meet with a psychologist. They wanted to be certain that we were all mentally stable enough to spend the next two years in Ecuador.

Two issues surfaced with me that became a regular part of the conversation with the psychologist. First, my girlfriend and I were talking quite seriously about marriage. I wanted to know if we could get married during my second year in the Peace Corps and live in Ecuador. This possibility was confirmed by the staff and by our in-country director because other members of the Peace Corps had married while serving. The second issue that the psychologist and I had to resolve was the concern about my loyalty to the United States of America. The concern was never stated that way, but it was not too difficult to read between the lines. What I didn't know was that as a part of the clearance process, the Peace Corps had sent someone to my old neighborhood in New Haven as part of a background check. In doing so, someone told them that I attended the weekly meetings of the Black Muslims and enjoyed listening to Malcolm X. The facts were true; Malcolm X did enjoy visiting New Haven because he enjoyed "sparring" with Yale professors. I told the psychologist that when Malcom decided to close the weekly meetings to everyone not seeking to join the Black Muslims, I stopped attending. I told several of my friends who continued to attend the meetings, that my Pentecostal roots were too deep for me to convert to Islam. It became clearer as we met that the psychologist was comfortable with my explanation and did not view me to be a threat to the integrity of the program. In other words, I would not be eliminated from the program because of this issue. But going through this process with her taught me a very valuable life lesson. People are watching and observing you even when you don't realize it, and under the right conditions will discuss and reveal your behavior to a perfect stranger. This could work both for and against you.

We were told that we would complete our training in Puerto Rico, and then head to Ecuador. After a week in a hotel in San Juan we were told that we would spend some time on the island with a family. We would be given the name and address of the household and sent on our way. We had to make arrangements on our own. The idea of course was that when we arrived in Ecuador, we would have to find our way to the city, find a place to live, and then locate our school. So why not try it out in Puerto Rico. I was assigned to a small town on the southern part of the island named Santa Isabel. My host was the superintendent of schools. Because of my comfort speaking the language, I found the process to be exciting and not scary. I hired a driver to take me from San Juan to the police department in Santa Isabel. I told the person in the police department that I had come from Ohio and was the house guest of Dr. Felix Vasquez, superintendent of schools. They called Felix and told him that I had arrived and was waiting for him at the station. He and his family arrived and took me back to their house. I enjoyed the week that I spent with the family. I had only seen Puerto Rico from the perspective of someone on the US mainland visiting one of the popular casinos. It was a real joy to see things from the perspective of someone living on the island. I spent the week coaching basketball at John F. Kennedy High School, and when I left to return to San Juan, I knew that I had made some lasting friendships. Some forty years later I took my wife to Santa Isabel to see where I lived during my Peace Corps training.

Soon after our return to San Juan, the Peace Corps training staff said goodbye to us and we were on our way to Quito, Ecuador, to meet our in-country director, receive a brief orientation to the country, and then sent on our way. The first night in Ecuador I got so sick that I thought that I was going to die in my hotel room. I had eaten pork chops for dinner because they looked and smelled so good. A few of us had forgotten the warning that we should avoid eating pork. I had never had a case of food poisoning before and have not had one since. The entire night, when I was not in the bathroom, I was curled up in a knot, holding my stomach. I never ate pork again while in Ecuador. As a proud Peace Corps Volunteer, I was assigned to a small fishing village called Manta in the Manabí province. My initial assignment was to coach basketball and teach physical education at a small Catholic middle school. There were two other Peace Corps Volunteers in the town, and they helped me find a place to live and arranged for me to buy my lunch and dinner from the same woman with whom they had eaten for nearly two years. They were extremely helpful and offered to let me stay with them, but I was afraid that if I lived with them, and spoke English all the time, I would not leave the country with the desired level of fluency in Spanish that I wanted. I used this example with my son Jack forty-four years later as he headed to South Korea to teach English. I warned him that if he spent too much time with English speakers, he would not master the Korean language as quickly as he desired.

Word soon spread around Manta that El Negro, as I was affectionately called, was in town and people had no trouble spotting me. I learned a lot about racial issues while in the Peace Corps. People in Manta called me Rey Pelé. Pelé is considered by many to have been the greatest soccer player of all time. He was a Black Brazilian, so to be called King Pelé was a sign of respect, but at the same time, a recognition of my Blackness. Sending me to the Manabí Province, as I would learn later, was no coincidence. This province had the highest percentages of Afro-Ecuadorians in the country. Unfortunately, I did not get to spend any time in the city of Esmeraldas which had considerable African influence in the culture and way of life. I thought it was funny to be asked if I was from Esmeraldas, but felt proud that I was speaking Spanish so fluently that some people thought I was Ecuadorian. Everyone had something for me to do. I had to remind them that I was there to work for the Peace Corps. First, a group of women asked me if I would translate a book for them. I agreed to do it before learning that it was a Spiegel catalog that they wanted me to translate into Spanish. In order to free myself from this "assignment" I moved immediately to the section that had some very personal items. None of these married women felt comfortable having such conversations with me, thus, my assignment was over before it started. Several of them would later approach me for help with purchasing items such as shoes, coats, and cosmetics. I was more than happy to help. I was also asked to teach adults to speak English. That assignment actually helped me with my Spanish, so I did a limited amount of tutoring. Finally, all the neighborhood children wanted me to teach them English. What I soon learned was that they only wanted to learn a few words that would allow them to speak to me in English, words such as football, hurry, ice cream, run, and hat.

It was in Ecuador that I realized how much we take for granted in the United States. I did a lot of letter-writing to my fiancée, my family, and some friends, so I expected to receive a lot of mail each week. The post office was about five miles from my house, and I walked there and back three times a week to check the mail or drop off a letter or card I had written. I used to explain to Ecuadorians that in the city of New Haven, we had a mailbox on every other corner and felt comfortable dropping something in the mailbox. They thought I was joking. Soon a few of the neighborhood children discovered that on the days that I went to the post office I stopped and had ice cream. They convinced their parents that it was okay to walk to the post office and back with Don Jaime ("Don" is a form of courtesy before one's first name; "Jaime" is James). Some days I would have as many as a dozen children walking with me to get my mail. I enjoyed it because I learned a lot of Spanish from the children, and they enjoyed the walk because they were going to stop at the Oso Polar (the Polar Bear) and get ice cream. What the children and their parents didn't know was that the owner of the ice cream shop wanted me to come to his shop so that he could quiz me to determine whether I was really with the Peace Corps or had been sent there by the CIA. He argued that I must be with the CIA because no Black American would travel to Ecuador to represent the United States given the way we were treated at home. He knew almost as much Black history as I did and wanted me to know that he had studied the lives of the great Black leaders of the 1960s. He also wanted to know if I was told by my government that he was a Communist. I responded that I knew nothing about him before arriving in the country. I don't know if I ever convinced him that I was an innocent Peace Corps Volunteer sent there to coach track and basketball, but I enjoyed eating his rum raisin ice cream and talking with him about what it was like being Black in the United States of America. The children were very patient because they were getting free ice cream each time they went with me. When the parents asked them why they were so eager to go to the post office with me, they said that "while Don Jaime and Mister sit and talk, we eat ice cream." Years later I would cringe at the thought that there might have been someone in the CIA among our group; and rum raisin is still my favorite ice cream.

The Volunteers in Ecuador received word that our director, David Carrasco, was leaving the Peace Corps to go to work in Mexico City as it prepared for the 1968 Olympic Games. We were all very sad to see him leave because he was a very good person, and a very good leader. He knew how to connect with people and was very popular with Ecuadorian officials. It was a double loss for me because he was the person with whom I had been talking about my fiancée coming to Ecuador so we could get married, and I would be able to keep my two-year commitment to the Peace Corps. Without going into all of the details, things changed after David left, and it was not too long after that that I left the program. We married on July 29, 1967, in New Haven, Connecticut, instead of Manta, Manabí Ecuador. I will always regret the way things happened. I enjoyed the Peace Corps and have since agreed to be a part of their recruitment efforts. I visited a couple of college campuses and high schools, and was on a video encouraging college graduates and others to consider the Peace Corps. As a result of my recruitment efforts, I was given a very special award at a Peace Corps Ceremony in Washington, DC.

Chapter 6

# DIVERSE INSTITUTIONS

## Diverse Challenges

I feel honored and blessed to have served as president of six minority-serving institutions, five of them historically Black colleges (HBCU) and one Hispanic serving institution (HSI). At the time of my appointment to the presidency of California State University, Dominguez Hills, I may have been the only person to have headed both of these kinds of institutions. When people talk about HBCUs, they often lump them together as though they are all the same. While many of the HBCUs may be similar in that they share a fairly common history, they have very different foci, and very different campus cultures. As a president, each university that I served required certain basic attributes that were necessary in order to be successful; but there were other attributes necessary to be successful in a particular environment. The issues also varied greatly at these institutions. Nearly all these campuses expressed a need for more funding, improved facilities, and infrastructure updates, but they each had their own issues. Some of the issues were discussed openly, others were the "elephant in the room." In this chapter I am going to share some of the challenges that I faced as the president. Some of the issues may surprise you but they were very real for me.

Bowie State University is one of a very few HBCUs that was in a white middle-class neighborhood at that time. That has changed now, but it was my reality. I wanted to figure out a way that I could take advantage of its location to bring much needed resources to the university. Was it possible for me to gain the support of our white neighbors, to generate resources for an institution that was described as a Black college? Was everyone comfortable with what some were calling "Black by day, white by night"? I really had no choice because it was not simply a matter of who attends during the day and who attends at night. The issue was how we were to provide the best we had to offer in order to guarantee student success, whether they took classes at 9:00 a.m. or 6:00 p.m. Graduate and continuing education were also an important factor. Many of our local residents did not want to drive to inner city Baltimore or Washington, DC, in order to take an education course. One afternoon I had a meeting with a group of local women who told me, in no uncertain terms, that they did not want to drive into either city to take courses that ought to be offered right in their community. The "Bowie Housewives" were ready and willing to go to Annapolis, the state capital, and fight for any new programs or facilities that were needed, as long as it included courses that they needed for certification or a master's degree.

It was very difficult to get some of the Black faculty and staff to understand that in a fight for resources, you use all the weaponry appropriate for the situation. Some of them feared that if the evening programs grew too strong, more white people would attend, and ultimately take over the school. I was able to convince most of them that this wasn't just about white people. We had to grow stronger and more competitive with other HBCUs as well. In order to increase our visibility in the region, I made a very strategic decision to lobby the mayor and our state and federal delegations to replace the Old Bowie Commuter Train Station with something more modern, and to locate it on our campus. They all liked the idea and joined with the campus to make it happen. This brought another three hundred people per day to our campus, and hundreds more admired the campus as the train stopped to pick up and let off passengers. One of the indirect results of this initiative was that it opened the campus up to Black students from Baltimore and DC who did not have motor vehicles. Our campus could now publicize our offerings more aggressively because students in both locations could now take the train to the Bowie State campus.

Another issue that was very real for me at Bowie State University was the fear, and at times paranoia, about being taken over by the state and merged with either Prince George's Community College or the University of Maryland College Park. During my first week on campus, I told some faculty members that I was planning to go over to the community college to meet the president. They asked me to consider changing my mind about the meeting because "those people over there want this campus." I explained that the campus had several thousand students and was our major feeder campus among all the institutions in the state. We had to have a strong relationship with them now and into the future. They responded by telling me that the University of Maryland College Park had long been interested in taking over our campus, and perhaps making it their freshman campus, so we had trouble on both sides: from a community college and from a major research university. When the state of Maryland put its support behind the development of a Universities Center in Montgomery County, this same group was convinced that this was the beginning of the end for Bowie State. They believed that it was created and supported to divert Montgomery County students from attending Bowie State. I encouraged them to offer a few Bowie State courses at the center to attract students from that county who might not be interested in driving to our campus. My argument was that when students met our professors and saw the quality of instruction, hopefully the word would spread that Bowie State was an excellent university.

I mention this personal challenge for me because outsiders don't always understand the challenges we face as senior-level administrators and presidents. In addition to all that we do as the campus CEO, we still have challenges, seen and unseen. This kind of challenge is real and is not to be taken lightly. Sometimes as presidents we make decisions that we would consider no-brainers, like building a new commuter train stop on the campus, only to find out that a certain percentage of your university stakeholders are suspect or fearful of the attention it may bring. This fear of being "taken over" or closed isn't just a Bowie State phenomenon; it exists at many HBCUs. There are HBCU campuses in states like Georgia, Pennsylvania, Virginia, North Carolina, Ohio, Alabama, and Texas that have similar concerns about being closed or merged, which presents a challenge for their respective leadership teams. I once asked a white colleague of mine how he would describe the differences between our two institutions. His response was that we are in the same system, have the same board, and have to deal with the same key members of the legislature, "but the main differences between your job and mine is that I have never spent one day worrying about whether my institution will be merged or closed!"

I have already said that the *United States v. Fordice* case was thrust into my lap before I could get in my car and drive to Jackson, Mississippi. However, there is an aspect of this case that was more challenging than people understood. A major source of confusion surrounding the case was that to the Black community the Fordice case was about the enhancement of Black colleges. However, to the state and the United States Supreme Court, the case was about desegregation. It was said on more than one occasion by some members of the Mississippi legislature that the case was not about making HBCUs "blacker and wealthier." When the state gave me money for new academic programs in response to the Fordice case, many members of the legislature expected to see evidence that we were successful in desegregating the institution. I remember contacting the head of a new program to ask how recruitment was going and she said recruitment had been very successful and the program would be ready to begin the following semester. When I asked about the number of white students in the program, I was told that there were none. I promptly informed her that I too was excited about the program because it was an important part of our urban mission, but I expected to be asked by members of the legislature, and by the judge, how funding for this new program had helped to desegregate Jackson State. They would want to know how many white students had applied and how many were admitted to the program. There was an expectation among my board members and members of the legislature that white students would be aggressively recruited and admitted to all the new programs that were a part of the Fordice case. This difference of perspective exists to this day whenever the Fordice case or similar cases are discussed. As an HBCU president I talked a lot about enhancing the Black college, knowing that if you have the right academic programs, offered in quality facilities, with appropriate resources undergirding the program, students of all ethnic groups will seek you out. In far too many cases the resources were not there in order to be attractive to all students. Mississippi's HBCUs had historically been forced "to do more with less." The Fordice decision was expected to change that narrative.

Another special challenge that I faced at Jackson State was the deteriorating neighborhoods in front of and on some sides of the campus. The night before my interview at Jackson State I decided to leave the hotel and take a walk. A security guard at the hotel cautioned me to turn left and walk toward the Governor's Mansion and avoid going up toward Jackson State. The next morning when I was picked up to be taken to the campus to meet with the search committee, it was obvious that the driver took the long way to the campus to avoid driving down Lynch Street. Later that day I told the search committee that I found it quite troubling that the area around the campus looked so bad that they did not want me, the candidate, to see it. After taking the position and selecting a church, one of the parishioners introduced himself and said that he was hopeful that as the new president, I would do something to enhance the neighborhood surrounding the university. He noted that his wife had to drive all the way to Hattiesburg, to the University of Southern Mississippi to pursue a graduate degree that was offered at Jackson State; however, she was afraid to come to the campus at night because the campus was located in the highest crime precinct in the state. He and his wife were Black.

Campus safety concerns were a big part of my reality while serving as president. It was a fact that our campus crime statistics were no different than any of the other universities in the state that were located in a city environment. However, the perception was that we were the most unsafe institution in the state. During one of our new-student orientation sessions, a parent came over to me to say that she was taking her daughter home because of the properties directly across the street from the honors dorm. She questioned why we would build the honors dorm in such a bad location. I convinced her to let her daughter stay by having her assigned to another building and promising her that I planned to do something about some of the areas near the campus. Finally, when a group of our students came to me and said that a man pulled a gun on their class during a "walk through the community" class activity, I knew that some action had to be taken before we had a tragedy on our hands. So, when I asked the legislature for money to purchase dilapidated buildings near the campus and extra dollars to build a new road from the campus to the center of town, a lot of people assumed and said that I was doing it because I wanted to attract more white people to the campus, and they would not attend Jackson State if they had to deal with the existing environment. The truth was that the first three people to ask me to do something around the campus to make it safer and more attractive were Black citizens of Jackson, Mississippi.

One issue that will always stay with me from Jackson State is the fact that the historical record of the Fordice, or Ayers Case as it is called in some instances, may show that I "turned down" the opportunity for Jackson State to have a medical school. I have been asked that question several times. As I look back in time, perhaps I was too much of a realist and much of this case was tied to the emotions brought on by neglect and in ·ome instances mistreatment of the Jackson State community. I found myself attempting to be practical and strategic in a very emotional environment. The attorneys for the plaintiffs had a medical school among their list of demands to settle the case. The University of Mississippi School of Medicine was already located in Jackson, not in Oxford on its main campus. As much as I wanted to see the number of Black physicians increased, given the size of Jackson, it was unreasonable to think that there would be two medical schools in the city funded with state dollars. That meant that the existing medical school would have to be taken from the University of Mississippi and given to Jackson State. I must admit that it sounded good and certainly would have gained a lot of attention nationally. Jackson State would join Howard, Meharry, and Morehouse as the fourth major HBCU medical schools on the east coast. After talking with a lot of people, I concluded that there was no way that the Mississippi legislature, composed of many "Ole Miss" graduates, was going to take the medical school from the University of Mississippi and give it to Jackson State. I conferred with many people, both Black and white; accreditors and other regulatory agencies; members of the medical profession; JSU alumni and non-alumni; business leaders; local elected officials, and members of the state's congressional delegation. Nobody told me that they believed it would happen. During the trial I was asked, point blank, if I wanted the University of Mississippi School of Medicine. I said no because I did not like the idea of taking programs from one campus and giving them to another campus. What would stop the state from taking one of our high-demand programs and moving it to Mississippi State, for example? The truth is I did not consider this a real offer; instead, it was a legal move to get me on the record.

My proposal was to build the strongest pre-med program in the country at Jackson State University. Given the proximity of the Jackson State campus and the medical school, there would be joint appointments of faculty so that undergraduates at Jackson State could be exposed to medical school faculty during their first year in college. There would be paid internships during the summer for JSU students, based on their field of interest in med school. These "JSU/UM Pre-Med Scholars" would have all expenses paid as undergraduates, guaranteed admission to medical school, all fees paid in medical school, and a mentor/tutor paid for throughout the program. Students who were interested in medicine or were pre-med students, not in the Scholars program, would receive many of the benefits of the program so that they would be very strong candidates for the med school of their choice. I still believe that this approach was viable and would have resulted in a tremendous number of Black physicians coming out of med school in Mississippi. My journey from Mississippi to California was next.

In response to the 1965 Watts Rebellion in California, Governor Pat Brown decided that a college was needed in this general area to serve the minority community. California State College, Palos Verdes, became California State College, Dominguez Hills, and was moved to the city of Carson. From its very beginning Dominguez Hills was created to serve the traditionally underserved. I enjoyed this mission and the opportunity that it gave me to tell our story. Our major benefactor at the time was Katherine Bogdanovich Loker. As an heir to the Starkist fortune, Mrs. Loker had the resources to donate to any causes of her choosing. She was a graduate of the University of Southern California and donated millions of dollars to her alma mater. The most important thing I learned from her was that a major benefactor need not be an alumnus of your institution. However, if that individual believes in your mission and what you are doing to make a difference in the lives of your students and your community, you have a potential partner. Such was the case with Mrs. Loker. She believed that we were doing "the Lord's Work" and she wanted to be a part of it. Her gifts to the university were very important and had an impact on our growth and development. She enjoyed teasing me whenever I approached her for support. Once I called her and indicated that I wanted to bring her a turkey for Thanksgiving. Her response was, "How much is that turkey going to cost me?" One of our fondest memories of Mrs. Loker will always be the evening she invited my wife and I to join her at "Le Grand D'Affaire" in downtown Los Angeles. We did not engage in any fundraising discussions that night; instead, we drank some of the most expensive wine sold in the USA. In fact, she asked if we wanted to book a room in the hotel so we would not have to drive home, having consumed a considerable amount of red wine. We declined the offer and drove home to Carson. The next day she called to see if we made it home safely.

Dominguez Hills was a completely different university from Jackson State. According to the US Department of Education, California State University, Dominguez Hills, is officially an HSI, Hispanic-serving institution. While its diversity is a strength, that diversity also presented some challenges. When I announced that I was moving to Los Angeles, it shocked a lot of people. Having worked at numerous HBCUs, it surprised people that I was going to a different universe of institutions. As I prepared to head to the west coast, I was advised by many friends who had lived there, that "people on the west coast are different." At times they would explain it and other times they said no more than that. I learned what they were talking about early on in my tenure. Before leaving the east coast, many individuals and organizations asked me to send them the date of my inauguration so they could prepare for the trip to Los Angeles. I promised that I would let them know as soon as possible. In a meet-and-greet session with a small group of faculty on my new campus, I made the comment that folks around the country were waiting for the date of my inauguration so they could buy airplane tickets early and save money on their trip to California. One of the faculty members said, "Mr. President, we don't do coronations at Dominguez Hills." I could not believe what I was hearing. Another indicated that he had served under two previous presidents, and there was no inauguration either time. Was the campus questioning why the first permanent Black president had to have a formal inauguration when the white presidents had not chosen to do so?

After the event was over, I called one of my predecessors at Dominguez Hills, who confirmed that he had not had an inauguration and none of the others had chosen to do so. I then called a few other presidents in the Cal State University system and learned that inaugurations were not as popular in California as they were in some other parts of the country. To have to tell the higher education community that I was not having an inauguration at Dominguez Hills would have been an embarrassment, especially after some of these same individuals and organizations had attended my previous ceremonies at Bowie State and Jackson State. One of the purposes for having an inauguration ceremony is to expose your institution to the rest of the higher education community and the general public. I wondered how I might get the idea across that I was not "hungry for a coronation." Besides, I had already experienced two of them and didn't have to have another one if it was going to upset the campus.

I decided to make it clear to the faculty that it wasn't about me; it was about Dominguez Hills. I explained that when a campus works on an inauguration, it is usually a wonderful coming-together of all the university stakeholders. If done well it could lead to additional national recognition of the campus and possibly be used as a springboard for financial support. Then I "swallowed hard" and indicated that I would delay the inauguration, and instead of having it during the fall of 1999, I would delay it until the year 2000, which would coincide with the fortieth anniversary of the university's founding. My investiture would be one part of a week of activities celebrating the institution's founding rather than a week celebrating the new president. This approach was accepted by most of the people on the campus, and we were ready to begin planning for the fortieth anniversary. I indicated that I would take care of the speaker, and the committee could plan all the other activities. Most of the ethnic studies groups and organizations saw this as an opportunity to showcase what they were doing and to let others in the state know that Dominguez Hills was alive and well.

Given that this was the institution's first such celebration, I wanted to make certain that the speaker would be someone they would never forget. So, I called a friend of mine in Montgomery, Alabama, and asked her if she would be the speaker for my investiture ceremony, and she agreed to do it. Dr. Tommie Stewart, former dean of the

College of Visual and Performing Arts at Alabama State University, would be someone that the faculty could relate to because she was one of them. In addition, they were getting an accomplished actress who played Aunt Etta Kibby on the television show *In the Heat of the Night*, starring Carroll O'Connor. She did such an outstanding job that even some of the naysayers admitted that they were happy that I pressed forward with the idea of an inauguration.

I went to Dominguez Hills looking for a way to distinguish it from the many institutions that were located in and around Los Angeles. This came in the form of a "once in a lifetime" opportunity to partner with a professional soccer team and move its home to our campus. As I looked at the Campus Master Plan, it was obvious that the university had far more land than it needed. I discussed this opportunity with my leadership team, especially the vice president for business and finance and the vice president for student affairs. The idea of building a soccer venue on our campus came about during a conversation between our athletics director and the coach of the Los Angeles Galaxy soccer team. The Galaxy played its home games in the Rose Bowl in Pasadena and didn't need that stadium's nearly one hundred thousand seats. The owner of the team and a couple of his staff flew over our campus to see how much space might be available for a thirty-thousand-seat stadium. Several weeks later we were invited to meet with Mr. Phil Anschutz, a billionaire businessman, and members of his staff, to discuss what we thought about having them build a soccer venue on our campus. However, when we met with them to discuss the stadium, they had a rendering of an Olympic training village with a stadium, a new running track, a velodrome, a tennis venue, and a hotel. They envisioned that the US Olympic Committee would send teams to the campus to train for the Olympics. For me the idea of partnering with a major sports and entertainment organization was a no-brainer. I informed their group that the campus was excited and would begin the approval process right away. But I had no idea how the nearby community would respond. When the announcement that we were planning to build an Olympic training site on the campus was made, the neighborhood erupted.

We had to get the board of trustees' approval for the planning to go forward. The team owner, Mr. Anschutz, was willing to use his own money to construct the venue if we signed a long-term lease agreement. At the meeting I informed the board of the financial arrangements, how much revenue would come to the university, how many jobs would be created, and that they would go to residents of the city of Carson first. I explained all the ways it would benefit the campus and the nearby community. After I spoke, local citizens were given the opportunity to speak. I understood some of the concerns because I lived across the street from the proposed site. What I was not prepared for were the lies and the anger. I had never been subjected to such bitter personal attacks in my life; some of them went far beyond the project itself and focused on me personally. "What kind of human being would build a soccer stadium in the middle of a quiet residential neighborhood?" one speaker asked. We later scheduled several public hearings in the community so that we could be very transparent about the project. I had to be given a police escort to a couple of the hearings. People even created T-shirts that said "stop the stadium." I was very disappointed when some of the people who testified against the project made it racial. Some folks in the African American community said that I was doing this to satisfy the Mexican community "because *we* don't play soccer." I reminded them of what it was like when African Americans began moving into Carson and had to stage marches led by the NAACP. I informed them that if this became racial, I would cancel the remaining hearings. I also reminded them that one of the greatest soccer players of all time was a Black man!

Based on the fact that the board of trustees had given us the go ahead, the Carson City Council announced that it would hold a public hearing before making a decision. For the city council hearing all the liars in the LA Basin must have been invited. They said that we should expect gang violence and possible deaths if first responders could not get through the traffic during a soccer game. They argued that home values would drop, vandalism would occur in the neighborhoods surrounding the campus, and the fireworks after the game would create an environmental hazard. We invited persons in the neighborhood who were in support of the project to attend the meeting so that the city council would see that there were people in the neighborhood who were in support of the venue. After much deliberation and discussion, the city council voted in favor of the project.

When we left the meeting at city hall, I had police protection to avoid any issues. Over the course of several weeks, there were conversations with neighborhood associations to discuss some of their concerns. We agreed to block off access to the neighborhoods on game days. Only individuals with stickers on their cars could enter the neighborhood. We agreed to provide pay to those who worked the check points. We interviewed Carson residents for the jobs that would become available when the venue officially opened. We worked with community groups to determine what type of events they would like to see held at the smaller venues. I even had dinner with two adult members of the most prominent street gangs in the neighborhood and discussed the project and what had been said about gangs should the venue be approved. One of the gang members laughed and said, "If we want to fight, we have the entire city of LA, why would we come over to Dominguez?" The project went through all the steps for approval, our university attorneys working with the builder's attorneys, and we finally got it done! The entire process was a learning experience and a very painful experience. There were times when I asked myself if the project was worth the beating I was taking. Didn't I have enough challenges just being a university president? Was the project really that important to the university? Did the local residents really understand that I was not doing it for myself? Shortly after the venue officially opened, word circulated throughout the LA community that I had been paid $200,000 for helping to guide the project to completion and had then left town. Obviously, they were wrong in both cases.

One evening Venus and Serena Williams were playing each other in a semifinals match at the venue. During a break in the game a woman stood up and turned in my direction and said, "Mr. President, I want to personally apologize to you for the way I behaved about this project. You said it, but I didn't believe that it would ever be possible for me to sit here in Carson, California, and watch Venus and Serena; and you only charged me ten dollars for the ticket." Her words brought tears to my eyes because they had put me through hell and she was apologizing! We had no gang violence, no one died as a result of the traffic, and the stadium restaurant became a popular lunch destination for Los Angeles–area residents. We decided to drop the idea of the hotel because we did not want to compete with local businesses. The 2003 Women's World Cup finals were held there on October 12, 2003, just four months after the stadium was completed. I can remember going into the press room and telling a sportscaster, "I understand why you are saying live from LA, given our proximity to the city, but would you say, just once for the world to hear, live from the campus of Cal State Dominguez Hills?" He promised that he would. The soccer venue did put us on the map because we were the only university in the country to have a professional soccer team make our campus their home.

One other factor that made Dominguez Hills a great place to work was the racial ethnic diversity of the campus. The campus student population was more diverse than any institution at which I had worked or attended. It really did look like America. The challenge for me was to figure out how to celebrate the diversity in a manner that would allow everyone to grow and not offend other groups. I had to get used to having a Black graduation celebration, a Chicano/a graduation celebration, and an Asian Pacific Islander graduation celebration. The events were great because there was a close connection to the community. Many of these students were the first in their families to finish college. The students were proud, and the families were proud, which of course made me proud to be in attendance as their president. My big concern was that these celebrations were not the institution's graduation, and students should not tell their parents that there was no need for them to attend commencement. Some faculty, staff, and students were not happy about my position, but they were in the minority.

I also learned that we had a Black student retention initiative and a Latino student retention initiative. I personally felt that they could have been combined because so many of the factors influencing retention were the same for both groups; however, that was not a priority for me at that time. Why create a major campus problem, and deal with negative reactions, when everybody was trying to help improve retention? While there as president, I encouraged other system institutions, as well as those in other parts of the country, to look at Dominguez as a model in higher education diversity.

When I retired as president emeritus from California State University, Dominguez Hills, I really expected that it would be my last presidency. I had worked in several different regions of the country and at several kinds of institutions. But when the president of Dillard announced to our board of trustees that she planned to retire at the end of the school year, the board asked me if I would step in for a brief time. I assumed the interim presidency in July of 2011 planning to remain until a new president was chosen to start in January. I was not a candidate. I jokingly reminded the board of trustees that I came to Dillard to serve on the board of trustees and not to be the president. I did not want to do anything as president that might anger them because we had to work together when I returned to the board. As it turned out, the successful candidate was a sitting president who could not leave his campus in mid-year, so I ended up serving until June of 2012.

The fact that Dillard, a United Methodist–affiliated university, is located in New Orleans, Louisiana, is both a plus and a minus. It is a destination for so many people who want to be there and enjoy the rich Cajun culture of the area. I probably have never eaten so much in a year as I did while living in the city. On the other hand, I spoke to some prospective students who felt that New Orleans was too much, too big, and too fast for them to go to school there. But they enjoyed visiting and attending Mardi Gras parades. Above all, a newcomer to New Orleans is struck by the lingering impact of Hurricane Katrina. As we know, Hurricane Katrina was a Category 5 cyclone that hit Louisiana, and particularly New Orleans, in August of 2005. It was reported to have caused $125 billion in damage. Dillard University was hit so hard that the campus was under water. There were even discussions about moving the campus to Atlanta rather than attempting to repair the damage. I was at Dominguez Hills when Katrina hit and called a meeting to discuss what we could do to help. We decided that we would reach out to students who had planned to return to a New Orleans school that fall or who were planning to enroll as first-year students. I told my senior staff that this was not an attempt to "steal" students from the New Orleans institutions. This was about trying to help sister campuses in a time of need. We had between twelve and fifteen students from Louisiana institutions that semester; two were from Dillard. Someone at Dillard came up with the idea of having students carry banners during commencement that spring with the names of the colleges and universities they attended during the fall semester. I must admit that I felt very proud when I observed a student walking down Dillard's famous "Avenue of the Oaks" holding up a Dominquez Hills banner.

The issue that has had a lasting impact from my service as interim president of Dillard was the lingering effects of Hurricane Katrina, both literally and figuratively. I was employed at Dillard in July of 2011, six years after Katrina, yet in some ways it was like the Hurricane just hit. The history of the city was now characterized by the phrase "before the storm." Whether you are measuring hotel occupancy rates or student enrollment, you are making comparisons based on what happened prior to Hurricane Katrina and since the hurricane. I am not even certain that residents of New Orleans hear themselves saying "before the storm" as frequently as they do. The remnants were both physically and emotionally visible. On campus we were still dealing with some Katrina issues. There were still parts of town that looked like a war zone, and there were other parts of town where you could see evidence that a rebuilding or renovation had taken place. When visitors came to town who wanted to see where the hurricane's destruction took place, I took them to two places. One location was just two blocks from my home. Two houses that were destroyed by the hurricane were still unoccupied and unfit for living without massive renovations. The second location was an abandoned church that still showed the water line indicating how high the water reached. One of my guests was a little over six feet tall, and the water line was above his head. It was unlikely that the church would ever be occupied again.

The lingering impact of Hurricane Katrina was also very emotional. Some people with whom I worked had relatives, friends, neighbors, and church members who died as a result of the storm. More common was the fact that so many people left town that it was hard to find a family that could not report a loved one who had not returned. In Atlanta there are still thousands of individuals who left New Orleans and remained in Atlanta. In fact, when the Atlanta Falcons play the New Orleans Saints in football, it is difficult to tell the home team because there are so many Saints' fans in the building.

New Orleanians have demonstrated tremendous resilience and are working hard to rebuild the city and its institutions. Unfortunately, Hurricane Katrina will exist in the hearts and minds of people in this city for years to come.

When I left Dillard in June of 2012, I returned to my home in Atlanta determined to remain at home with my wife, and really retire this time. I had been successful at it for about six months, when I received a call asking me if I knew that the University of the District of Columbia (UDC) was seeking an interim president. The caller explained that my work at nearby Bowie State University, and my stint as secretary of higher education in Maryland, might be attractive to the members of the board of trustees because they would understand I had DMV (District of Columbia, Maryland, Virginia) experience. I indicated that I had been interested in UDC years ago but decided that the fit wasn't right. The district government was too heavily involved in the day-to-day affairs of the university, and I did not want to report to a board of trustees and a city council. He encouraged me to think about it and if interested call and speak with the chairlady of the board. I discussed the matter with my wife, and she encouraged me to go for it. After all, we had lived in Maryland for a total of thirteen years and had spent a lot of time in the district. We reasoned that it might be fun to live in a city where we had spent so much time visiting. I contacted the board chair in December, and we had a very pleasant conversation. She said that the board would like to have the interim person on board in January. After doing my own due diligence I called the chair back and told her that I was available for an interview. Either the interview went very well or they were desperate, because I was offered the interim position. We chose to live in the Newseum Apartments on Pennsylvania Avenue. My wife and I enjoyed holding rooftop receptions, which was a popular thing to do in DC. Living so close to the action was fun except when then-President Obama decided to leave the house. The DC police would block all of the streets to allow the president's motorcade to pass. On one occasion the president had a speaking engagement next door to our apartment building. The Secret Service took over our building two days prior to the event. In fact, all residents were required to open the trunks of our motor vehicles on the morning of the event so they could be inspected. If you had to go to work, they expected the car to be unlocked and the trunk open.

I arrived on campus concerned about the role of the mayor and the city council in the ongoing affairs of the university. It seems as though colleagues from around the country had heard about the city government meddling in university affairs. I understood that UDC was quite unique because the DC City Council created the university in 1977 when DC Teachers College, Federal City College, and Washington Technical Institute were formally consolidated as the University of the District of Columbia. Then in 1996 it merged the District of Columbia School of Law with the new University of the District of Columbia. So given the evolution of the university, I understood the sense of ownership that the council and the mayor felt. As one who had studied higher education governance, I found myself explaining to the mayor and individual members of the council when I thought they were crossing the "oversight" line. Sometimes they listened and sometimes they didn't.

Another unique factor about working at UDC was the fact that the president of UDC is also a member of the mayor's cabinet and is often referred to as a department head. While I did not like the idea of getting email from the mayor addressed to department heads and directors, I did not let it bother me. While I understand that some of my predecessors may not have liked the idea of having to attend cabinet meetings, I looked forward to them because everybody in city government that I needed to see was at the meeting. If I needed to speak to the director of health, I knew he would be at the meeting. If I needed to speak to the school superintendent, I knew she would be at the meeting. From time to time, I had to remind the mayor, privately of course, that I wasn't exactly like the other members of his cabinet because I reported to a board of trustees that he appointed. As the university began to talk about accreditation and our relationship to and the expectations of the Middle States Association, our accrediting body, I felt the necessity to try and schedule a meeting between the university leadership, Middle States' leadership, the city council leadership, and the office of the mayor. I knew that Middle States had heard a lot of negative comments about political interference and government overreach regarding UDC. Much to my surprise, I was able to schedule what turned out to be a very positive and constructive meeting. Everyone spoke candidly about how they viewed governance and what Middle States expected of colleges and universities in its region.

A good example of this peculiar relationship between the university and the city occurred when it came time to renew my contract. After the board of trustees had approved my new contract, I was told by the president of the city council that I had to have a hearing before the city council for them to approve it. To me this was a very serious violation of best practice in higher education governance. To make matters worse, the public was free to come and testify at this televised hearing. Who ever heard of a university president having a televised hearing with the city council to discuss his employment contract after the board of trustees had already approved it? I was very concerned that should this process be communicated to Middle States, our board of trustees might receive some sort of sanction. I met with the president of the city council and explained that this procedure violated everything that I understood about governance in higher education, and it would get the board in trouble. So, I told the president of the city council and the chairman of my board of trustees that I would not be able to attend my reappointment hearing because I had to be out of town that day; they both understood. The evening went off without a hitch. The chairlady of the board attended the hearing, and witnessed my contract being approved by the city council.

While I served as the interim president of the University of the District of Columbia, the city mourned the loss of then-city council member but former Mayor Marion Shepilov Barry. One afternoon I received a call from him telling me that he was the best friend that I had on the DC City Council, and he wanted to do more for the university. I responded by telling him that I just saw on television that he had been rushed to the Howard University Hospital. He said that he was still there but needed to talk with me. Later that evening the television reported that he was in ICU. I was left to wonder why he cared so much about UDC that he would call me from intensive care. Mayor Marion Barry, the "Mayor for Life," died on November 23, 2014.

After spending the Fourth of July in DC, I left the city and returned home to Atlanta, a year and a half later than expected. This time I was sure that my days serving as a university president were over. Back in Atlanta I was enjoying retirement with the family and helping my wife get her new career as an artist off the ground. In March of 2017, nearly two years after returning to Atlanta, I received a call from the Registry, an organization that may have been the first of its kind to place retired college and university presidents into interim positions. They informed me that a request had come to them to place someone on an interim basis at Concordia College Alabama. The Lutheran Church Missouri Synod had decided they were not going to continue funding the institution. They were willing, however, to provide resources to help bring about a "dignified closure." I told the folks at the Registry that I had spent my entire career trying to build and strengthen institutions and I had no interest in going to close one. I thanked them for thinking of me and the conversation ended. A few weeks later I received a second call from the Registry indicating that the local board of trustees had identified an investor who was interested in taking control of the college if things could be worked out. This investor had already made a payment substantial enough to be taken seriously. After a very long and serious conversation with my wife, I decided to take the interim position to work with the college to try and save its wonderful legacy. So, in May of 2017 I got in my car and headed to a place that I had heard so much about: Selma, Alabama. I had never dreamed I would live in such a well-known city, and yet I was headed there to be their interim transition officer. Unbelievable!

Concordia College Alabama was the only Black college in the Concordia University System, a part of the Lutheran Church Missouri Synod. It was nearly a hundred years old and indeed a legacy to Rosa Young, a Black woman who convinced the church that even the poorest of Black Alabamians needed to get an education. The Lutheran Church was so inspired by her work that it produced a movie called "The First Rosa." The jacket of the DVD calls it a "film that will enlighten the church about Rosa Young's remarkable history, initiate and invoke the vocation of new professional church workers, and inspire the establishment of new Rosa J. Young Academies." I was honored to have been asked to help maintain this legacy and to help keep this Lutheran college open.

From May to September, I worked tirelessly trying to help the investor put things in place so that he would feel positive about assuming control. I met with state and local officials, the US Department of Education, and representatives of our regional accreditation commission, the Southern Association of Colleges and Schools (SACS), in an effort to touch all of the bases, to make this change of control happen. One item that was raised more than once was whether an international group from Taiwan could assume majority control of an American, regionally accredited institution. That was not the most immediate concern of the investor. Two major concerns of his were that we continue to reduce expenses and that we started an online MBA program. I could tell that the latter was a very high priority for him. This was probably because he knew that there was a market in Asia for an accredited MBA degree from an American institution. This program would surely help him recoup some of his investment. I traveled to Atlanta from Selma for a meeting with our SACS liaison to discuss the possibility of offering an online MBA degree. We would have to go through a substantive-change process because of the new program and a new degree level. We agreed to start the process by scheduling a date for a "special visit" and hiring a consultant to work with us on the structure of this new degree program.

The one thing that we had no control over was what the investor was doing to put together his investment group. He simply reported that he was working on it. During one of our call meetings with the board of trustees, the investor indicated that he was having trouble putting his group together. He indicated that he might not be able to do what he had promised. This was very unfortunate news for the college because we had such high hopes that the investor would keep his word and the institution would be able to remain open. The word began to circulate around the campus that the investor could not deliver on his promise. Barring an unexpected multimillion-dollar gift, he was the last option we had to keep the school open for the students, faculty, and staff. There were so many rumors circulating that one could see things heading in a downward spiral. When I heard that a group was deliberately spreading the word that we were going to close the college during the Christmas recess and "leave everyone hanging," I decided to call a campus-wide meeting.

At the meeting, attended by faculty, staff, students, and some alumni, I explained that the institution was having serious financial problems, but we were not closing at Christmas time, and we would never treat them so cruelly. If we should have to close, I promised that I would schedule another meeting to inform them before anyone else. It was clear to me by that time that I was going to have to do what I told the Registry I did not want to do: oversee a "dignified closure." As we prepared to leave campus for the Christmas holidays, my senior staff and I knew that we had cut the budget to the point that such action was no longer an option. If the church was still unwilling to provide the support necessary to keep the doors open, this would be our last year. Needless to say, it was a very sad Christmas holiday for all of us. When we returned after the new year it was no longer a question of if we were going to close, but when. In fact, there was a concern that we might run out of money before the end of the semester. We decided to notify the appropriate regulatory agencies that we would probably have to close the college at the end of the semester. We did not want them to read about it in the newspaper. I committed to working with each of them to do what was necessary to carry out an orderly closure. Without a lot of fanfare and discussion, I scheduled a campus-wide meeting for February 21, 2018. At that point everyone probably anticipated what I was going to say to them. A student reminded me that at the December meeting I said that if I called us all together again, the news was not going to be good.

Throughout my career I have had to address some very difficult situations, but nothing like this. As I walked across the street to the meeting, it seemed as though the building was a mile away. It was the longest walk of my career and the most difficult moment in my more than fifty years in higher education. After having spent a whole career trying to build institutions and make them more academically competitive and sustainable, I was about to stand in front of the entire campus community and tell them that there would be no more Concordia College Alabama as a place to work, teach, or study after June 30. As I spoke, I could feel the pain that my words were causing. There was a wide range of emotions from the audience; some people were crying, some gave a resigned shrug of their shoulders because they believed this was coming, and some were angry because they didn't know what they were going to do. The board of trustees had worked as hard as it could to keep the institution open, exploring every possibility until the very end. My leadership team, the faculty, and the staff were hard at work right up until the very end. They didn't abandon their responsibilities because we were planning to close our doors. I explained what we were going to do to be of assistance to them, to help them move forward in the future. Together, with the staff that remained, we did all that an institution must do when it decides to close. A year and a half later I was still writing letters of recommendation for some faculty and staff who were my colleagues at the time. This experience really took a toll on me. This will be my last presidency, permanent or interim!

# Chapter 7

# 1400 JOHN R. LYNCH STREET

In 1986 a book written by Robert Fulghum got everyone's attention because of its title, *All I Really Need to Know I Learned in Kindergarten.* I cannot say that all I needed to know I learned at Jackson State, but I can say that some of the experiences I had, both professionally and personally, influenced me as a leader and as a person, as I would go on to assume four more presidencies.

I was offered the position at Jackson State with a start date of July 1, 1992. I was very excited about the move to Jackson and started working on my "First 100 Days" list. But something historic happened that made me think about tossing the list into the proverbial trash can! On June 26, less than one week before my scheduled arrival in Jackson, Mississippi, the United States Supreme Court issued its decision in the *United States v. Fordice, Governor of Mississippi, et al.* case. This lawsuit was filed in 1975 by private plaintiffs led by Jake Ayers. Many in Mississippi refer to the case as the Ayers Case. The court ruled that the state of Mississippi had not dismantled its historic dual system of higher education, one white and one Black. It noted that:

> The courts below did not apply the correct legal standard in ruling that Mississippi has brought itself into compliance with the Equal Protection Clause. If the State perpetuates policies and practices traceable to its prior de jure dual system that continue to have segregated effects, . . . and such policies are without sound educational justification and can be practicably eliminated, the policies violate the Clause, even though the State has abolished the legal requirement that the races be educated separately.

On remand, the State was directed to look at all its policies, determine whether maintaining eight institutions was contributing to the problem, and consider the funding of the three historically Black universities in the system. So rather than spending my "first 100 days" focusing on internal matters, I spent them being "schooled" on the lawsuit. As I looked back at my experience in Mississippi, much of what I did on a weekly basis was related either directly or indirectly to the Fordice case. I spent a lot of my time talking with the attorneys who were representing the state of Mississippi and with Alvin Chambliss, one of the lead attorneys for the private plaintiffs and a Jackson State graduate.

One important lesson that I learned while at Jackson State was how sensitive people are when personal friendships are involved. When the NCAA began taking student athletes' academic progress more seriously, I did not want to be caught unprepared, so I enhanced the position of the student academic advisor in the Athletics Department, and with the concurrence of the athletics director, appointed a former graduate school classmate of mine to the position. To make matters even more interesting, his nickname was Jughead. I considered it a great fit because he had a doctorate and the appropriate academic credentials, had taught on campus, loved intercollegiate athletics, and he loved the students. I sent him to an NCAA meeting to learn the ropes so that the institution could remain in compliance with NCAA policies. Others on campus felt that it was a good position for "your friend." Things went along quite well from the NCAA perspective, and I was pleased, but I was told that the word was spreading around campus that my friend wasn't doing anything during the day but taking cigarette breaks. I knew that work was being done because I had to sign off on certain things, but if people were making that assumption, it wasn't good. I had never appointed anyone before that would be considered a personal friend; even though I did not hire him at Jackson State, I did give him this new assignment. I called him and asked if we could meet to discuss his performance. Upon his arrival he asked if I had called him to my office to fire him based on rumors that I may have heard. I told him that it was not my intention to fire him, I just wanted to clear the air. I told him that as "the president's friend" he was under a lot of scrutiny, and it was important to me that he demonstrate a strong work ethic and be viewed as the hardest-working person on the campus. That was the price he had to pay for being my friend and placed in a position that others may have wanted. We had a very good conversation, and it had a real impact on me as I considered making future hires of anyone who might be considered a friend. Rightly or wrongly, there is added pressure on anyone identified as the president's friend. There is a saying: "Perception is reality." Although he went outside to smoke a cigarette a couple of times a day, to the people on campus "he was always outside smoking." He continued to do the job very well, and I had no reservations about sending him to NCAA meetings as a Jackson State University representative. Shortly after I left Jackson State and moved to California, he was removed from the position. Another lesson learned!

One question that I was asked quite frequently was how I felt working in the shadows of the university's sixth president and alumnus, Dr. John A. Peoples Jr. Given some of the horror stories that people have heard about the relationship between the sitting and the former president at some institutions, there was a lot of curiosity. I admit that when I arrived on campus and heard that he sometimes attended alumni meetings and would speak his mind, I had some trepidation. But all of that went out the window after meeting him for the first time. He was willing to spend as much time with me as I wanted or needed. There were things that he shared with me that would have taken three years to discover. He later gave me a copy of his book *To Survive and Thrive*. I wanted to learn as much as I could from Dr. Peoples, and he let me know that he was available if I needed to see him. In my opinion, he is truly the favorite JSU president of all time. I would model my behavior of dealing with a former campus, and its sitting president, after Dr. Peoples. I have tried to make it clear that I am as close as the telephone, but far enough away so as not to interfere. I think this approach has been appreciated by most of the presidents that I have preceded.

Based on comments that I have received over the years, my legacy at Jackson State University will always be associated with the Fordice case, the acquisition of property near the campus, and the development of the Campus Master Plan. On more than one occasion while traveling

I have met Jackson State alumni who recognized my face but couldn't remember my name. They usually mentioned one of these three items to make it clear that they really remember something about me. But what is missed about my seven years at the university is the personal, human-interest side of my stay in Jackson. For me personally, it wasn't just about the professional achievement of being chosen to take the helm of one of the most well-known historically Black universities; in addition to that it was my experience as a man, husband, father, and colleague moving from the northeast to the Deep South. During my interview on campus, I remember being asked if I had ever lived in the South before, and I said yes. When I indicated that I had lived in North Carolina, the person who asked the question responded that North Carolina wasn't the South, it was up east. That was an eye-opener because it made a statement about how the individual viewed things from his Mississippi perspective. Therefore, on a very personal level I feel that this story, my stay at Jackson State, is about moving from one culture to another, not just an educator moving from one position to another. On numerous occasions I was given lectures about how things were done in the South. But Jackson State, being located in the South, was just a part of the issue. The fact that it was in Mississippi was at times a real issue. As a university president, I enjoyed my time in Jackson; however, I am mindful of the fact that there are still negative perceptions about the state because of its history.

When the word spread around higher education circles that I was headed to Mississippi, I received many congratulatory calls and emails. But what was different this time was the fact that only one person asked to go with me, and I wasn't sure that he was serious. In every other employment situation, I have had people ask to go with me, or say, "Keep an eye out for something I can do." In this case it was the exact opposite; in fact, I received calls from friends and colleagues asking me if I was crazy, or if I was losing my mind. Just the mention of the word Mississippi seemed to evoke an unbelievably negative response that I did not receive when I mentioned that I was going to North Carolina, Delaware, Maryland, or the District of Columbia. I was sure that the negative responses I received after the announcement had more to do with the history of the state of Mississippi and the images it had built up over time than it did Jackson

State University. Once I arrived in Jackson and had a chance to meet members of the Jackson Chamber of Commerce, and other business organizations, I told them what I had experienced. Much to my surprise, I was told that they had heard it before from people moving in from other parts of the country. One person mentioned a businessman who was sent to Jackson by his company to help build its brand in the South. He said that people in the company actually asked him, "Who did you piss off at corporate to be sent to Mississippi?" The whole time I was there I talked about the importance of a national PR campaign for Mississippi. There was a real image problem for the state, and I offered to do whatever I could to help it improve.

As I prepared to head to Jackson, I made a staffing decision that some will second guess forever. I asked my assistant to the president/ chief of staff at Bowie State if she would join me at JSU. Dr. Kathleen Walton had a very serious discussion with her sons and decided to make the move. When a white female showed up for work in the president's office at Jackson State University, rumblings were heard throughout the state of Mississippi. There were other white faculty and staff members working at Jackson State, but not in the president's office! I did not ask her to join me because I wanted to be a martyr or because I was trying to make a social statement. I did it because I really wanted to be sure that there was someone on campus who had my back, whom I knew I could trust. When I introduced her to the senior staff, they were very cordial. My cabinet embraced her, and soon others on the campus did too. Because of our age difference, the campus did not think that she was my girlfriend; so, they spent their time asking the question "who is she going to replace?" She had been a professor of English, a graduate school dean, a provost, and an assistant to the president. Assumptions were made about which of the incumbents on campus was about to lose her/his job. Unfortunately, they wasted their time because I had not planned to give her any of their positions. Her only purpose for leaving Maryland and coming to Mississippi was to help me do what I had promised to do, take JSU to the next level. While she was there, a number of situations stand out in my mind that I am sure became lasting memories for both of us.

On her first day on the job, we completed what we considered to be a successful day and decided to leave things until the next day. As we exited the administration building headed to our cars, shots rang out across the street. I nearly knocked her over attempting to push her back inside. We stood inside the lobby while I called the campus police to ask them to go and check on what was going on. They reported that the gunfire came from the crack house across the street. I can honestly say that that was the only time during my seven years at Jackson State that I asked myself whether I had made a mistake taking the job. Did I have to call the police every time I was leaving the building heading to my car? Would I have to call the police just before leaving the office each day to ensure that I would not be struck down by a bullet? How could I build a first-class urban university in a neighborhood where you might get shot walking out of the administration building? I am certain that Dr. Walton was asking herself the same questions. I am also certain that she did not call and tell her sons what had happened. They would have demanded that she catch the first plane headed to Baltimore. Several years later a white businessman spoke to me privately about heading up a fundraising campaign to build a new campus in another part of the city. He even agreed to donate the land. He told me that his concern was not related to race; it was related to the perception that Jackson State is in a very unsafe location and may never reach its full potential with the main campus located in West Jackson. I understood the point that he was making but moving the campus to the fairgrounds or another downtown location was not the answer. I did not accept his offer.

Another story relating to Dr. Walton is equally interesting. We had been at an all-day meeting at Mississippi Valley State University, our first time in the Mississippi Delta. I suggested that we visit a catfish farm so I could take some photos. The catfish industry was so important to the state's economy that I wanted to share photos with my friends. We noticed signs indicating that a catfish farm was nearby, so we drove there, got out of the car, and started taking photos. A white man walked over to us and asked our purpose. When I told him what I was doing he took the time to explain the catfish industry, and what it took to develop a farm like his. He was very cordial and would have talked longer if we had not been ready to leave. We thanked him and drove away. On our way back to the main road I stopped at a grocery store to get a couple of bottles of water. One of the Black men sitting in front of the store noticed Dr. Walton in the car and asked me where I was from. When I said Jackson, he indicated that he meant where was I really from. I told him Connecticut. He advised me that we were in Mississippi and that I should not feel so comfortable riding around the Delta with a white woman in the car. I thanked him for his advice, purchased the water, and returned to the car. It was an important reminder to me, notwithstanding the friendliness of the catfish farm owner, the many white friends and acquaintances I enjoyed in Jackson, and the fact that it was 1992, there was still one obvious reality: we were in Mississippi. I never discussed what he said with Dr. Walton, but his words echoed in my ears for a long time.

As we drove through the Mississippi Delta, I was struck by the fact that at one point, as far as the eye could see in either direction, there were cotton fields. If the human eye can see a distance of three miles, that was a lot of cotton. Cotton used to be picked by hand, so it helped me understand the slave trade in economic terms. The owner of that property would have needed hundreds of slaves to pick that much cotton; and it was just one location, in one county, in one state. Right there in the car I could just imagine the number of slaves needed throughout the South to keep this enterprise going. I had been given two history lessons during that one trip to the Delta. Fortunately, or unfortunately, the learning opportunities continued.

On another occasion I was in the city of Gulf Port, Mississippi, with my son Jack and one of his friends. We stopped at a store that sold snack food and ice cream. While waiting for our ice cream, we noticed a man standing in front of the restrooms with his back toward us and outstretched arms. Soon his wife and daughter emerged from one bathroom and his son from the other. I wondered whether this man was blocking the doors so that we could not enter the bathrooms. Of course, we would not have gone into the lady's room anyway. As it became obvious that he was "protecting" his family from us I jokingly said, "sir, I am the president of Jackson State University here with my boys. I have never hurt anyone nor killed anyone, so you don't have to worry about us." I will always remember his response: "I haven't killed nobody either . . . yet!" He was not joking, and I could see that, so we decided to leave the store immediately, to avoid any trouble. I don't remember whether we picked up the ice cream that we ordered.

The important thing to me was to leave the store and head back to Jackson.

During the ride back home, Jack and Justin expressed their anger. I told them that they had every right to be angry because what just happened made no sense. This man really felt like he had to guard the bathroom doors to keep us from entering. However, I took the time to make it a "teachable moment." I told them that when you are dealing with racism such as we just encountered, logic goes out the window. The man did not see a university president with a PhD. What he saw was a Black man that he did not want to get too close to his family. The second lesson that I communicated to the boys was that no matter how much we enjoyed living in the cosmopolitan city of Jackson, and no matter how friendly people of all racial and ethnic groups had been to us, no matter how much he enjoyed most of his classmates at St. Joseph Catholic High School, we lived in Mississippi and some things had not changed! That I would not forget. Some twenty-five years later I heard Jack talk about his first trip to Gulf Port, Mississippi. He obviously will never forget that experience.

After two years on the job, Dr. Walton was notified that her leave status had changed, and she was expected to return to Bowie State for the next academic year. After her departure, a senior faculty member said to me, "We blew it. We were focused on whose job she was going to take, and not on the fact that her only purpose for being here was to help you to help us make JSU the best university possible." Over the course of the next several weeks a number of faculty and staff members acknowledged that they missed a real learning opportunity because everyone was so suspicious about her reason for being there.

One afternoon while pumping gas I received a good lecture about living in the South. A member of the Jackson State campus police force happened to drive by and saw me doing what I have always done when my fuel was low. He made a U-turn and came back to the station, got out of his car, and came over and introduced himself. He then asked, "What are you doing?" I wanted to say something funny like, "You don't appear to be visually impaired, what does it look like I am doing?" But he was so serious that I didn't joke with him. When I responded that I was going out to explore the town and decided to leave home on a full tank of gas, he said that was fine, but "the president of Jackson State doesn't stand out here pumping gas. . . . It looks bad." He was referring to the police department and the university as a whole. I told him how much I appreciated his concern, but I had just completed nine years at another university, and nobody was ever surprised to see me pump gas or go to the carwash. He said that it doesn't work like that in the South. Up north they may not care, but in the South, we love our university president, and it is a pleasure to serve him. "Whenever you need something like this just call the department and someone will take care of it for you." At that moment I felt like I was in a classroom taking "Living in the South 101." After thanking him for stopping to be of assistance, I got back in the car and left for my tour. This would not be the last time that I did something that was not done in the South.

To assist me with another concern I had, I asked the director of public safety at Bowie State if he would be willing to come to Jackson State as a consultant. He was surprised that I would extend this opportunity to him, but he agreed to do so if I needed him. I had already witnessed a few things that caused me concern. I gave him some general background information about the city and the university. I also shared information about a few incidents that occurred on or near the campus. At my own expense I asked for a situation report and recommendations. I wanted an outsider who knew nothing at all about the university to take a look. I told my team about it and explained that I wanted to bring myself to a certain comfort level about campus safety. I wanted to be sure that we all had a safe place to work, study, and live. I reminded them that I lived on Lynch Street. My consultant came to town, worked very hard walking the campus day and night, and talked to students, faculty, and staff. During his work he learned of some incidents on campus that I had not heard about. I could not have paid him for all the time he put into this undertaking. He gave me a briefing on the report and headed back to Baltimore. I shared a copy of the final report with the campus chief of police, who generally concurred with its findings. One of the most important findings to me was that the campus had far too many points of entry and unless the police department doubled in size, there was no way to cover every location. The corresponding recommendation was that we consider fencing in some or all of the campus.

I knew that my decision to build a fence of any kind would be controversial, but it was a battle that I was willing to take on. As a parent, I would want to know that the university was doing all that it could to make the campus a safe place. I was also reminded that I lived on the campus directly behind the science building and was impacted by whatever happened in the neighborhood. One night I was walking my dog on campus, and she got away from me and ran under some shrubs. While in the bushes attempting to retrieve her, two female students exited the front door of the science building. It was late at night, and they were doing some work in one of the science labs. I allowed them to walk a few yards away from the building, then I came out of the bushes and called them, identifying myself as Dr. Lyons. I asked them if they had seen or heard me before I called out to them, and they said no. When they asked where I was, I was hesitant to tell them because I did not want them to be fearful, and they really should not have had to worry about someone jumping out of the bushes, with or without a dog.

The next day we did a campus walk around and I directed that they cut down anything that could conceal an individual who might be up to no good. I also asked that lights be replaced in places that needed to be better illuminated. Two days later some members of the staff expressed their displeasure with me for cutting down the shrubbery in front of the science building. It just confirmed that no matter what you do, there will be some folks who will find fault with your actions. I discussed my plans for the campus with an attorney who wisely pointed out that once the report was given to me it did make me liable should something happen. A parent could point out that "your own commissioned report said that you needed additional police officers and you didn't hire any, if you had done so my child would not have been robbed." That really convinced me to go on and erect a fence in some locations and take other actions, no matter how unpopular, to help secure the campus.

I had not yet met the publisher of the *Jackson Advocate*, but I knew that he could be very harsh toward people that he either didn't like or didn't respect. Every week he had what he called the "Brown Society," and if you were listed, he would criticize you in a very harsh and sometimes cruel manner. I decided to go and introduce myself to him, not as the president going to speak to the publisher, but as one Black man to another, both of whom were concerned about the welfare of the Black community. We had a very good conversation. I told him that I wanted him to be the first to know what I was doing and why. I said more to him than I had to my staff about what had happened and what I feared might happen in the future if I didn't take this action. I had photos of other area colleges to document that none of them were exposed like we were. We ended the conversation cordially, and I left thinking that we were on the same page. When the plans for a fence became public, I was surprised and hurt by some of the negative reaction. I asked myself how anyone could believe that this "colored man from the North had come to Jackson to lock up southern Negroes, so they can't get out!" I was given several suggestions about the fence. One concern was that the members of the community walked through the campus in the morning to go to work, and this would hinder their access to public transportation. So, we had a gate put in where the community members were taking a shortcut across the campus. It was opened early in the morning and closed late at night. As is so often the case, the individuals who approved of my actions said very little, leaving the impression that everyone in Jackson was opposed to the fence. After some tumultuous days and sleepless nights, and numerous personal attacks about the fence, things settled down. To this day, I still believe it was the right thing to do. The most important thing to me was to do whatever I could to help insure the safest possible environment for all who studied, worked, and lived on the campus.

Another situation occurred at Jackson State that was very personal and received state and national attention. It caused a lot of pain because it was, in my opinion, a deliberate attempt to gain public attention at my expense. It grew out of a mandatory property audit. All state agencies must conduct a physical audit of their property. When the Jackson State audit was conducted, more than $100,000 of inventory was reported missing. My contention from the very beginning was that we had a records management problem rather than a theft problem. If the football players were to carry a broken washing machine out to the dumpster, but it is not officially removed from the dormitory inventory, it would show up missing. If a department

chairman gave a coffee table to a colleague down the hall because he
had a new table coming in that afternoon, and it was not removed
from the former's inventory list, it would be reported missing. However, the state auditor at the time, Steven Patterson, decided to deal
with the matter as though everything missing had been stolen. Some
of our alumni said that he was politically motivated and wanted to
use me as an example. I was able to document that the computers
"missing" from the School of Business were donated to the nearby
middle school, which allowed them to create a very excellent computer lab. Unfortunately, they were never removed from the campus
inventory. I also documented for the press that a few pieces of items
"missing" from the president's house were in the student center. Most
people understood what was happening and stopped highlighting it
as a news story.

But the auditor took the matter to another level. He decided to
make a personal demand for the money from the president of the
university. He used a law written decades earlier that allowed the
auditor to make a personal demand on the agency head for the money
to cover missing inventory. I was the agency head. The money was
to be delivered to the attorney general of the state of Mississippi. In
response I pointed out that everyone in the state knew that I had not
stolen any furniture or equipment. I had not stolen anything at all,
so I was not going to spend one dime on lawyers defending myself
against such craziness. I indicated that "I would rather go to jail and
while there write a screenplay about the incident." I will admit that
the idea of going to Parchman prison did frighten me. Rumor had it
that cell blocks sometimes reached 130 degrees.

Many citizens throughout the state asked how they could help.
They wanted to send me money to resolve the dispute. While I appreciated their generosity, I could not receive any money because of
a potential tax liability. In order for individuals to donate, a fund was
established. I had no control over the fund and did not know how
much had been collected. The fund was called the James E. Lyons
Education and Legal Defense Fund. The president of the Jackson
State University Foundation had the authority to withdraw money
and deliver it to the attorney general. This matter went on longer than
any of us expected. Again, because it was happening to me, it took

a toll on my family. One morning on the school bus a child said to my son, "I don't want to sit beside you because your dad is stealing furniture." I had to explain what was going on to my sons. Even an employee at a nearby recycling site went on television and said that JSU employees come to his place all the time selling items. He made the six o'clock news. His moment of fame!

While all of this was going on, Bernie Ebbers, CEO of WorldCom, was paying attention. We had spoken many times before about a variety of things. He invited me to breakfast one morning at a place called Franks. We discussed my desire to see Jackson State be more of a workforce engine for central Mississippi. With the right programs and the support from the legislature, I knew that we could be a force, a sort of model urban university. He was following the media discussion about the audit and had some concerns. He concluded that the "missing inventory" debate was taking too much of my time away from the task for which I was brought to Mississippi. He wanted me to focus on graduating the best students that we could so they could be employed by local businesses and industry. One afternoon I received a call from his office to come visit him the next morning. In his office he repeated that this inventory problem didn't make sense because I had documented that the problem was record keeping and not theft. He told his secretary that he wanted to make a contribution to the fund, at whatever amount was needed to end this "madness." He asked that I keep it confidential. I gave them the name of the person who was handling the fund because I didn't know what was needed. He understood why I should not be involved.

The word soon circulated that the attorney general had received the money and this saga was over. Everyone wanted to know who paid the money and of course I would not say. Much to my surprise, one of the reporters from the *Clarion-Ledger* wanted to know if Bernie Ebbers paid the money, but I refused to discuss the matter. Perhaps he thought there was only one person in town who had that kind of money. I really had no idea why he asked that question. Although Mr. Ebbers asked me to keep his contribution confidential, which I did, he would later have to reveal the information himself. Rev. Jesse Jackson had announced that at the next WorldCom shareholders meeting, he was going to discuss the fact that WorldCom was not doing anything to benefit the Black community, and it had the resources to do so. A couple of weeks prior to the shareholders meeting I received an invitation to attend the meeting and to be prepared to make comments if necessary. I considered sending in regrets, but how could I after what Mr. Ebbers had done for me? So, I confirmed that I would be in attendance. I was also made aware that he had invited several other individuals, including some members of the clergy whose churches had been vandalized or burned down. It was clear that when Rev. Jackson made his claim, Mr. Ebbers was going to point to us as examples of what he had done for the Black community, anonymously. The night before the meeting I located Rev. Jackson and told him that I needed a few minutes of his time.

I have known Rev. Jackson for many years. I told him that when he made his comments about WorldCom at the meeting, there would be a number of us who might be called to set the record straight. As a friend, I did not want to be put in the position to have to contradict him in a public meeting. He appreciated my "heads up" but said that just because Mr. Ebbers had done a few things, it didn't take WorldCom off the hook. When Rev. Jackson spoke at the meeting, he did qualify his comments based on what he had learned from me. I was not asked to make a public statement and was grateful for that. The shareholders meeting went well with both Mr. Ebbers and Rev. Jackson feeling good about it.

After the money was paid to the attorney general and the audit was officially closed, the university continued to work very hard to improve its record keeping. Every time a piece of property was moved, the appropriate entry was made on the inventory form. A couple of years later, then state auditor Phil Bryant contacted me in California to share the news that JSU had a perfect audit! He mailed me a certificate that was made to congratulate Jackson State for the perfect audit. He knew that right up until the time that I left the state, I was working with staff to rectify this problem. Incidentally, about ten years later the previous state auditor, Mr. Patterson, who had made the personal demand on me for the money, and had spent weeks criticizing the university, was sentenced to two years in prison, and fined $150,000 dollars for his role in a bribery scheme. The judge who sentenced him, Judge Biggers, was the same judge that I had to appear before after the Fordice case was remanded to his court in Oxford, Mississippi.

# Chapter 8

# PRESIDENTS ARE PARENTS, TOO

There are a lot of people who don't consider the fact that many of us who carry the title of CEO or president are also parents. I must admit that sacrifices are made as you try to meet the 24/7 obligations of the job, and at the same time fulfill your responsibilities as a parent. I know that at times my sons have felt like they were being raised in a single-female-headed household because I was not there. There are times, however, when the role of father trumps that of president. For example, while preparing to move to Mississippi, I learned that soccer was played at the middle school level. Jack was a very good soccer player, so I used this to help excite him about the move to Jackson, Mississippi. Soccer was not played in public middle schools in Maryland at the time, so it gave him bragging rights. But shortly after arriving in Jackson I learned that you had to be in the eighth grade to participate. Needless to say, I was very unhappy about that news because Jack was in the seventh grade and had been playing soccer for several years. When I discussed this matter with school personnel, I learned that the decision was made to avoid sixth and eighth graders playing football against each other. The potential physical difference in football is something that you can understand, but why was the decision made for all sports? When the word spread that I was very unhappy about this matter, a couple of parents approached me and asked if I would take this to the school board. These parents were upset that their sons could not play football and said that if the president of Jackson State got out front on this issue, the policy might be changed. I explained to them that this issue had nothing to do with Jackson State. It was about a father who had promised his son he would be able to play soccer in middle school, only to find out that it was not true. I expressed a willingness to write a letter, but it would be coming from the father of Jack Lyons, and not the president of Jackson State. I wrote the letter, and in it I pointed out that while football may be a legitimate concern, there are other sports such as swimming, track, and soccer where the physical difference may not be as much of an issue. My efforts to make it clear that I was writing as a "soccer mom" notwithstanding, the word on the street was that the Jackson State University president was critical of the school board's policy on athletic participation.

There are also times when our children have to deal with the fact that their parents are public figures. When our son Jimmy learned that we were moving to Jackson, he started exploring opportunities for himself. When the Jackson Public School District learned that he was an art major at North Carolina A&T, he was invited for an interview. There was a shortage of art teachers in the district, and even though he was not in teacher education, they felt that he had the skills to teach elementary-school students. While his heart was actually in law enforcement, he realized that this was a good opportunity for him. So, when they offered him a position that would require him to teach at two elementary schools, he accepted the job. I was proud of our son. He had worked very hard at A&T, and this was an opportunity for him to follow in the footsteps of his parents because we both started out teaching in the public schools. I did caution him about the fact that having a dad in such a high-profile position would become a part of his reality. I am glad that I pointed this out to him because there was one incident that actually went "over the top."

One of his young students was misbehaving, so he told him to stay after school. He planned to counsel the student and let him know that certain conduct would not be tolerated in the classroom. When the boy's father learned that he was being kept after school he went to the classroom. As my son was attempting to explain why he kept the child after school the parent refused to listen and instead said, "Just because your father is the president of Jackson State doesn't mean that you can treat my child this way." Fortunately, the principal intervened before things got totally out of hand. Jimmy saw firsthand that having a father who is the local university president could be both a blessing and a curse. I felt terrible that this happened, but I had no control over the situation. I wanted to contact the principal but decided that it might make things worse. I wanted my son to have a successful tenure as a

classroom teacher like his mom and his dad. He did a good job with
the children, but soon, his first love, law enforcement, came calling.

When our middle son Jamal learned that his brother had accepted
a position in Jackson, meaning that four of us would now be living in
Jackson, he too decided to explore things at Jackson State. Jamal was
a freshman business major at Hampton University in Virginia. With
the whole family now in Jackson he wanted to come and "check it
out." I learned that Jackson State did allow a student who was in good
standing at his home institution to spend a semester as a "visiting" or
"transitional" student. I told him that he could spend the fall semester
at Jackson State, but it was his choice. I told him that his tuition would
be in the bank so that when he decided to return to Hampton there
would be no financial issues. I really wanted to make certain that he
was doing what *he* wanted to do. My concern as his father was that
if I seemed to be encouraging him too much, the decision could
come back to haunt me years later in the form of "I wanted to stay
at Hampton, but you made me transfer to Jackson State." I remained
at a distance from the process. Deep down inside I viewed this as a
kind of a litmus test for Jackson State. I saw no reason why he would
not stay at Jackson State if we did all the right things. We had a strong
program in business with very competent faculty, the campus itself
looked nice, and the fall semester had football and homecoming.
In late November he asked me if I thought that he should return to
Hampton, and I told him if that was where he was happiest, he should.
He also asked about the business major at one university versus the
other. I informed him that they were both likely to be accredited by
the same body, and both universities were accredited by the Southern
Association. Just before the Christmas break, he told us that he had
decided to remain at Jackson State. I am sure that it was a very tough
decision because Hampton was an extremely popular university and
there would be lots of questions about why he transferred. I applaud
him for making a very difficult decision at that point in his life. Now
the entire family was in Jackson, Mississippi. My wife was teaching
at Hinds Community College, Jimmy was working for the Jackson
Public School District, Jamal was a student at Jackson State, and Jack
was a Jackson Public School student. As parents we were very happy
to have everyone together under the same roof again.

Anyone who has young adult children will understand this next event. I was talking on the office phone with a member of my staff when my mobile phone rang. I answered it only to learn that Jamal had been stopped while driving through McComb, Mississippi. After running a check on the tags, they took him to jail. My staff member advised me to go to McComb immediately because tomorrow they might tell me that Jamal committed suicide by hanging. It seems that there had been a few other cases where Black parents were given that explanation. I certainly didn't want to be one of them. Needless to say, I ran out of the office and probably broke a speed record driving the seventy-six miles from Jackson to McComb. It is amazing what can go through your mind under such circumstances, and all of it was bad. I did not understand why anything negative would show up when they ran the tag numbers. I didn't have any fines or unpaid traffic tickets, so what could it be? When I reached the police station everyone was very nice. I introduced myself as James Lyons and expressed shock that this had happened to my son. They had already checked me out and responded to me as Dr. Lyons. I was told that my son was driving through McComb with the music blasting and was pulled over. When they ran the tags, they discovered a warrant from Maryland. It turned out that I had not properly filed the forms to have my Maryland tags and registration canceled, and therefore owed the Department of Motor Vehicles some money. After the sergeant and I discussed the matter, and he informed me that he looked forward to attending Jackson State, my son and I left. As I drove back to Jackson, I couldn't decide whether it had been a good night or a bad one. My son had been stopped for "driving while Black," but as a result I learned that I had an outstanding debt in Maryland. Jamal also learned that the loud music he was playing in the car attracted attention that could have had a tragic ending.

One morning while sitting in my office I received an urgent call from the campus police asking me to come there as soon as possible. When I arrived, I saw our youngest son Jack sitting there and immediately knew that something was wrong. He had been robbed of his saxophone, his shirt, and his sneakers, while standing in front of the house, waiting for the school bus. I felt terrible on the one hand, and thankful to God that he was not physically injured. The robbers wanted his instrument, but decided that they liked his shirt and sneakers as well. The Jackson Police Department moved quickly to contact all of the local pawn shops to be on the lookout for a male and a female suspect who may try to pawn a musical instrument. The story made the evening news, and it appears that our son was not the first child to be robbed of his instrument while waiting for the bus. I received a call from a very irate parent who really should have placed her call to the police department. She fussed at me about the fact that her child was robbed a couple of weeks earlier and nothing was done until the son of the Jackson State president was robbed. Now it was on the evening news and everyone was concerned. I allowed her to continue until she decided to tell me that she was sorry for the way she had spoken to me. I assured her that I was concerned about her child too. It was the worst form of violation to be robbed, standing in front of your home waiting for the school bus. It wasn't too long before an alert pawn shop owner had a visit from someone trying to pawn a saxophone. He followed them outside and was able to write down their tag number. A short while later the pair was arrested and taken into custody. When Jamal heard what had happened to Jack, he drove up from New Orleans and joined Jimmy as they drove around Jackson looking for the couple that had robbed their little brother. My wife and I were so happy that the police found the pair before our sons did. We still hate to think about what could have happened if Jimmy and Jamal had found them first.

The mother of the young lady who was arrested had the nerve to call my office and ask if I would call the police and ask them to release her daughter so that she could return home to her infant child. I jokingly said to her, "Let me shift the phone to my other ear because I want to be sure that I heard what you said. You want me to call the police department and ask them to let the woman who pulled a gun on my son, took his instrument, shoes, and shirt, go home to be with her infant child?" She responded that if the president of Jackson State called, they would do it. I asked her where her infant granddaughter was while her daughter was out robbing children of their musical instruments? I told her I would not make the call to the Jackson Police Department and hung up. What nerve!

Mississippi higher education is organized similarly to many other states. The governing body is the Board of Trustees of the Institutions of Higher Learning (IHL). It has eight members from all over the state. Many of them have attended one of the public institutions. The board appoints the commissioner of higher education to carry out its policies for the eight universities. The eight institutions are Alcorn State University, Delta State University, Jackson State University, Mississippi State University, Mississippi University for Women, Mississippi Valley State University, the University of Mississippi, and the University of Southern Mississippi. University presidents worked directly with the commissioner and his staff, but we also enjoyed a good working relationship with most of the board members. I do not know much about how things were at board meetings prior to my arrival in 1992, but I can confirm that there was a lot of activity, especially surrounding the states' response to the Supreme Court's decision. I recall a very action-packed board meeting involving our students. A young student activist from Columbia University, who was working for the *Jackson Advocate* at the time, encouraged the undergraduate students to become more active. This resulted in a rally outside of the IHL office. Some of the students entered the meeting and presented their concerns; however, they refused to leave the meeting after presenting them. When I overheard a call to the police, I quietly pleaded with the students to leave before the police arrived. Some listened to me and left the board room, and others refused. It became clear that a decision had been made by some to go to jail if necessary.

That was exactly what happened. Several students were arrested and taken to jail for refusing to leave the board's meeting. That night I received a call from a parent who was calling from out of town because her daughter was in jail. I informed the mother that I would get out of bed and go down to the jail and check on her daughter. She asked if she should wait before flying to Jackson. I told her that my goal was to get all of them out of jail in the morning. Even though I pleaded with the students to leave the meeting, I had to put myself in the position of their parents. If you are in Chicago, and your child is in jail in Jackson, you are worried. I spent the entire night in jail with the students. Although I had advised the students to leave the meeting several hours earlier in order to avoid being arrested, there

I was that night behaving like a parent, going from one student to the other so that I could reassure their real parents that things were okay. All the students were released the next day, which made it unnecessary for any of the out-of-state parents to rush to Jackson. At the same time, I had some very productive conversations with some of the students and their parents about activism and protests. It was a teachable moment that I wanted to enjoy. The young man who encouraged their activism ran for governor of the state of Maryland about twenty years later.

Things were going quite well at the university when our LLC was asked to compete for a contract at the Jackson Airport parking facility. In retrospect I should probably have declined rather than risk any turmoil on campus. At first, I was hesitant because I did not want to risk criticism from another company that was bidding for the contract. They might publicly ask how the JSU president could run the airport parking operation. It was a management contract for the successful bidder. The airport authority maintained all the rights, and more importantly the money, that the successful bidder would collect. I agreed that Mississippi Parking Associates should bid on the contract. One of the reasons that I did it was because with all my sons now living in Jackson, they could all have a job at the airport and perhaps develop an interest in entrepreneurship. Much to my surprise we won the contract, and my son Jimmy was named the manager. I told my campus leadership team before they read it in the news. I assured them that I had my priorities in order and there was no need to worry. I explained what a management contract was and how things would operate.

Things went quite well, and I felt good that Jimmy was able to hire his brother Jack and later students from Jackson State and Tougaloo College who needed money for school. I should have known that things would not run smoothly forever. At one of the airport commission meetings, it was mentioned that they were a multimillion-dollar-a-year operation and growing in a positive direction. Someone misunderstood the concept of a management contract and assumed I had a million-dollar business at the airport while serving as president of Jackson State. Someone even introduced the idea that for us to hire Jackson State students was a conflict of interest. Imagine how

I felt directing Jimmy not to hire anymore Jackson State students. But I did so to avoid even the appearance of a conflict of interest. I knew that even though I started out trying to do the right thing for the right reasons, this project could not last as long as I had hoped it would. After the contract expired, Mississippi Parking Associates didn't compete for a renewal.

There are times in life when something is dropped in your lap and you don't even know how it happened. In 1996 I was notified that I would be one of more than twelve thousand people who would be in the Olympic Torch Relay leading up to the Atlanta Olympics. There is no way to describe the joy and excitement that I felt after being asked to do so. I soon had another surprise coming because I would light the torch on stage at a Jackson music festival, while the Mississippi Mass Choir was singing. Then I would leave the stage and run past the Governor's Mansion and hand the flame off to a high school runner. I had driven past the mansion many times but hadn't thought about the fact that the street was on an incline, and I would be running uphill. I didn't want to pass out while running to make my exchange, so I started practicing running up the street. My sons encouraged me to do some running and even went out to practice with me as I ran past the mansion, to test my stamina. Even my doctor asked me to stop in for a physical because he didn't want me to fall out in the street and have to identify him as my physician. I think he was serious.

When the day came, I was ready to go. As the music started, I made my way to the event, already dressed in my Olympic relay shirt. I met the Georgia state trooper who would lead me off the stage, through the crowd, and down the street. I informed them that my son Jack would be running with us. As the Mississippi Mass Choir began to assemble on stage, I took my place behind them. It was an honor to be on stage with the Mississippi Mass Choir on this occasion because I had a very close relationship with the organization and several of the choir members. In fact, when Jackson State renovated its auditorium, the Mass Choir was the first group or organization scheduled to use it after the reopening. They produced an album that night with Rev. James Moore, "Live at Jackson State." I was very anxious but managed to calm done once I arrived backstage. Then it was showtime. As the choir sang, I walked out on stage, took the torch, and lit it to the roar of the crowd. As I approached the first step off the stage, I nearly stumbled because there were so many flashbulbs that my vision was blocked. As I ran through the crowd, with Jack running behind me carrying a flag, all I could see was the back of the state trooper's shirt and flash bulbs. When we reached the street, I was able to see where I was going, hold the torch up high, and run like an Olympian. As I ran past the Governor's Mansion, I knew that I was doing okay. I reached my destination and handed the torch to the next person. My part was over; it had been a great evening, one that I shall never forget. I owe it all to Jackson State University.

# Chapter 9

# PREPARATION

As I look back over my life, I sometimes try and count the number of students to whom I have spoken. If you consider the number of university commencement events, the number of commencement addresses I have given at other institutions and high schools, the number of honors programs, back-to-school convocations, career days, and the like, I probably have spoken to tens of thousands of students and young people during my fifty-plus years in education. That is quite an audience. Each time I spoke I challenged them to use the talent they had been given, to set goals for themselves, to work hard to achieve those goals, and as Rev. Jesse Jackson used to say, "Don't let your attitude determine your altitude." This may very well have been my purpose, and God equipped me for that challenge. Dr. Charlie Nelms, in his book *From Cotton Fields to University Leadership*, identifies four attributes that he says nothing is possible without, while with them anything is possible. He identifies aspirations, preparation, hard work, and mentorship. It may very well be that I have possessed the right number of these attributes over the last seventy-eight years to have achieved a certain measure of success; and I hope that I have passed them along to those who have heard me speak, or to those that I have mentored.

As early as the seventh grade I worked hard. I had two jobs when I was in junior high school, one in the morning before school and one in the afternoon. I was convinced at an early age that hard work was the only way to advance myself and improve my situation. Perhaps watching my mother and my father-in-law instilled a strong work ethic in me. They set the right example for me. Mom worked all day and then came home and took care of us and the apartment. My father-in-law, who was a physician, worked in his office all day, then made the rounds to see his patients, who were in the hospital or nursing home, and then did house calls at night. So, I can easily check off the hard work box that Dr. Nelms mentions. Aspiration is a very important attribute. If you have no goals in life, if you don't want to accomplish anything, then odds are you will not. Long before the US Army coined the phrase "Be All that You Can Be, in the Army" I wanted to be all that I could be. At one point I aspired to be an officer in the Air Force and was willing to put in the hard work to make that happen. That is important; you may aspire to do great things, but if you are unwilling to put in the hard work and then prepare yourself, your aspirations may be no more than dreams. I can check box number two.

At every stage of my journey, I made certain that I was prepared. If I had not worked hard enough in high school to prepare myself well, I would not have been admitted to college and the story of my first week at UConn may never have materialized. Or, if I had not worked hard as an accreditation team chair, and been willing to accept some very difficult assignments, my credentials in this area would not have been strong enough to capture the attention of the personnel at the California State University system. A check for box three. Finally, having a mentor, or someone who plays that role, is more important than many people realize. I was blessed to have had mentors throughout my life and career, even if they did not understand the important role they were playing. They included a sixth-grade English teacher, a high school Spanish teacher, a visiting professor from Spain, and my major advisor in graduate school. All of these individuals cared about me and believed in me. They saw something in me that made the "investment" of their time worth the effort.

There is one item that Dr. Nelms did not mention, that I must mention because it had a lot to do with my journey. For me, having a supportive wife is a factor that greatly influenced my life and my career. I am aware that it is customary for every writer to thank his spouse or partner. That is appropriate and the right thing to do. However, in my case I am talking about a loving and caring wife who made great personal and professional sacrifices to help me advance in my career. My wife Jocelyn, whom we call Joy, is a sociology graduate of Wilberforce University in Ohio. She earned a master's degree in education from the University of Connecticut, and a second master's degree in theological studies from Spring Hill College in Mobile, Alabama. Her first job out of college was as a case manager with the Department of Social Services in Philadelphia, Pennsylvania. After a very dangerous encounter in one of the neighborhoods in South Philadelphia, she left the department and became a public-school teacher. Her career as a public-school teacher, an elementary-school principal, a community college instructor, and as a religious counselor, was successful by any metric used to gauge her performance. When it was time for me to pack up and take another position, she packed her bags, even when it meant leaving family and career options behind. For example, when we left Philadelphia to move to Storrs, Connecticut, she left behind a grandmother and a host of aunts, uncles, and cousins, whom we had enjoyed so much. She had also just left the Department of Social Services to start an elementary-school teaching career. In a brief amount of time, she was demonstrating that she had a special gift for working with young children. When I left Fayetteville State University to go to Barber-Scotia in Concord, North Carolina, she was a day-care center director working with the Army Corps of Engineers, who were building a child-care facility on the site of a low-income housing development. In addition, we had just purchased our first home and she was enjoying the fact that we were putting down some roots. But she agreed to leave because it was a promotion for me.

When I left Barber-Scotia College and headed to Delaware State College, she was serving as the Cabarrus County day-care coordinator in charge of construction and certification of all day-care centers. Any person in Cabarrus County who wanted to start or build a day-care facility had to get her approval. This was a job "to die for," one of the most prestigious in county government. When we left Bowie State to go to Jackson State, we had recently moved out of the president's house on campus and into a new home. She was also teaching at Prince George's Community College and directing its Study Skills Lab. Finally, when we left Los Angeles California to return to Maryland, she was employed as the director of the Afro-American Center for Evangelization for the Catholic Archdiocese of Los Angeles; and worked part time in campus ministry at Verbum Dei high school in South Central Los Angeles. Verbum Dei was an all-boys Catholic Jesuit school that served students from South Central who were academically and economically underserved. I often tell a story that highlights the success my wife was having in the archdiocese. We were attending a very big reception in Los Angeles, and I was standing behind her as we proceeded through the receiving line to greet Cardinal Roger Mahoney, the archbishop of the diocese at that time. When we reached the archbishop, the person doing the introductions said, "Your Eminence, I would like for you to meet Joy Lyons' husband Jim." That really showed me who was the most important person that evening. As many times as she has been introduced as Dr. Lyons' wife, she has never said anything to make me feel uncomfortable.

The point that I am attempting to make is that my wife made decisions that helped advance my professional career, even when it affected hers. There were several times that she could have argued that we should not move because of the significance of what she was doing, but she didn't. I know a colleague in California whose career may have been impacted by the fact that he and his wife have accepted the reality that they both have professional careers that they are pursuing and do not intend to limit each other's career opportunities. At one point he was interviewing for a university presidency, and the search committee asked whether his wife would be joining him if he were offered the position. His response to the committee was that she would be on campus as often as her job allowed, but that she would not be leaving her tenured position at a university in northern California to join him on campus. Another former colleague was interviewing for the position of provost. She was a very strong candidate but did not get the job. The feedback that she received from the firm was that conducting the search suggested the president may have been concerned that if her husband was not planning to relocate with her, she would probably be commuting home more often than he would like. After the process was over, she jokingly asked me, "Should I not acknowledge that I am married when I go on my next interview?"

This is a problem or challenge that many professional couples have to face, and they must make the decision that is best for them. I have been blessed with a wife who put her career on the back burner to support my move through academe. I will forever be grateful.

Chapter 10

# THE VALUE OF THE JOURNEY

So how do I end a journey that began in 1943 and ends in 2020? A journey that starts with the Mafia fighting with the Communists, a trip to college with only the clothes on my back, then on to South America, to the United States Supreme Court, from there to the Olympic Torch Relay, and finally in front of a campus community announcing that the college would be closing at the end of the semester. And then there were stops along the way that either directly or indirectly influenced the journey, especially the stops on North Eagleville Road in Storrs, Connecticut, and JR Lynch Street in Jackson, Mississippi. There were also many forks in the road that could have sent me in a different direction or ended the journey all together. I will always remember that night at the gala banquet in Beverly Hills when the maître d' asked me, "Does everything meet your expectations, Dr. Lyons?" Did he know that he was talking to the high school student who accepted catering work at Yale University so that he could bring some of the leftovers home to his family? Did he know that I told people in my high school that my middle name was Earlington because James Earl sounded too "country," but on my first job in North Carolina I was proud to tell them that I enjoyed the name James Earl because it was really southern? Did he know he was talking to a young man who went off to college with the clothes on his back, and had to use the dorm laundry room each night to wash clothes for the next day? Did he know that he was talking to the young man whose pastor's acknowledgement that he was on a trip kept him from going to jail? Could he be expected to understand that I was the little boy who shined shoes in front of the Yale University dining hall, and years later returned to that same building as a guest university president? Did he know that he was talking to a young man who might never have been sitting at that head table if his heartbeat had been just a little bit slower? Did he have any idea that the man sitting before him at the table had a Graduate Record Exam (GRE) score that was low enough to have kept him out of the PhD program, and probably out of a presidency?

Did my classmate Joan see something in me when she wrote in my high school yearbook, "Good luck Mr. Lyons, remember me when they award you the Nobel Peace Prize"? Or Sharland who wrote, "Jimmy, best of luck to a fine language scholar"? Is it possible that these two classmates saw something in me that I didn't see in myself at the time? Have I come to the end of this journey with more questions than answers? It was truly a long road from Dixwell Avenue in New Haven, Connecticut, to Broad Street in Selma, Alabama. Leaving Dixwell Avenue with such a desire to go to college at the University of Connecticut that I arrived there with only the clothes on my back, and fifty-seven years later leaving Concordia College after announcing that it was closing, denying similarly situated young men and women in Alabama the opportunity that I was given. Or maybe, and this may sound trite, in the final analysis it isn't about where you started or where you finish, but what happened in between.

The national alumni president of one of the institutions where I was president called and invited me to attend the homecoming boat ride. A surprising number of alumni had signed up for the dinner cruise, and he thought that it would be a great reunion if I were available to attend. I liked the idea and indicated that I would attend the event. Once on the boat I really took advantage of not having to be center stage. The university president was not on the cruise, and I wondered how it would be received when he heard that I attended the alumni event. But that didn't diminish the joy I felt engaging with former students. Of course, I was asked to make some remarks, which is typical at events like this. My remarks were brief, simply highlighting how appreciative I was of having been invited and how much I enjoyed spending the evening with them. As I was returning to my seat a man approached the podium and said, "Point of personal privilege," to the alumni president. The president told him to go ahead but be brief because they wanted to sing the alma mater before the boat docked. The young man said, "I want to say something tonight that no one has ever heard me say publicly. Dr. Lyons, you don't know it but when you put me out of school my freshman year for smoking weed in my room, you saved my life!" He went on to tell the crowd that he was hanging out with the wrong people and doing the wrong things as a first-time college student. It appears he was attracted to everything that was bad and repulsed by everything good. He then said, "Dr. Lyons, when you told my mom and I that I should stay home until I was ready to be a serious college student and to take advantage of this opportunity to make something out of my life, that was the best thing that could have happened in my life."

At that point he became very emotional. There wasn't a dry eye on the ship. "You told me that when I was ready to be serious about my future to come and see you, which I did." As tears began to roll down his face, he told everyone that he came to see me, and we had a conversation that was more like a father and son than a university president and student. He was readmitted to the university, and in his own words, "I never looked back." As he returned to his seat, he said once again, "I just wanted to tell you that you saved my life." I got up, walked over to him, and hugged him. I congratulated him for his successful career and then said, "Your story is my story. That is why I do this work."

Over the past several years, I have frequently been asked, "How did you determine when it was time for you to step down or retire?" More often than not, this question has been raised either by a sitting president or by a presidential aspirant seeking to understand the whole truth about being a college or university president. Some of these individuals were presidents who were growing weary from the hectic daily routine; others were individuals who were concerned about a deterioration of their health; while some others were concerned that they were falling out of favor with their board and might need to be planning an exit strategy. My answer to all of them, and to others who may find themselves similarly situated, is that there is no standard answer. This is a very personal decision and is made after serious consultation with your spouse and others, as appropriate. There are many factors that must be considered such as age, health, personal finances, tenure status, and employment contract language. This wasn't as traumatic a situation for me as it is for many others.

When I assumed the presidency of Bowie State College, now Bowie State University, I was thirty-nine years old. I reasoned that even if I worked there for twenty years, I would still be young enough to do something else. So, I began my career with a clear understanding that for me, there would be life after the presidency. The only question for me was under what circumstances my decision would be made. The question was answered for me when I accepted my contract to serve as president of California State University, Dominguez Hills. As a part of that letter of appointment, I was granted a university professorship and tenure in the School of Education. I was fifty-six years of age at the time and knew that I would be sixty-six if I remained at Dominguez Hills for ten years and chose to teach after the presidency. During the 2006–2007 academic year, I made the decision to retire. I enjoyed all three presidencies and had worked very hard to move each institution to its next level of excellence. I had served more than twenty years in higher education as a campus president and was now ready to step away from this role.

As I began to talk more freely about retiring, the word somehow reached the newly elected governor of Maryland, Martin O'Malley. The governor was still assembling his cabinet, and I was informed that there was an interest in speaking with me about the position of secretary of higher education if I was really planning to retire. I flew to Connecticut to spend a couple of days with my mother before going to Maryland to meet with the search committee, which was chaired by Lt. Governor Anthony Brown. While in Connecticut my mother was rushed to the hospital. While sitting in her hospital room I received a phone call from the governor's chief of staff providing me with the logistics for my visit to Baltimore for the interview. I informed him that I was in my mother's hospital room, she had been admitted due to congestive heart failure, and I would not be able to travel to Baltimore at that time. He understood and asked that I contact him with a new date as soon as possible.

When I finished the call, my mother started a series of questions. Were you talking with someone about a job? Do you think they will hire you? Is the job in the state of Maryland? When I answered yes to all three of her questions, she said "Call that man back and tell him that you can take the train down to Baltimore in the morning." She indicated that she would rather have me in Maryland than in California, so I needed to go to the interview. I called the governor's office back and told his chief of staff exactly what had happened. After a good laugh we discussed the interview process. Rather than announcing I was leaving the CSU after twenty-three years as a university president and looking forward to retirement, I announced that I had accepted a position with the governor of Maryland. My wife told the governor that he could have me for his first term of office, but after that I had to join her in retirement. After helping him campaign successfully for a second term, I left Maryland headed to Georgia and retirement. Three interim presidencies later (Dillard University, University of the District of Columbia, Concordia College Alabama), I actually retired.

Even in retirement I have kept busy doing consulting work on my own and as a senior consultant for the Association of Governing Boards of Universities and Colleges (AGB). I am enjoying working with AGB as we address governance in higher education. The engagements have taken me all over the continental USA, to Puerto Rico, Kenya, and the United Arab Emirates. Each campus has been quite different but shared a desire to improve governance. I hope to continue this work as long as I can make a real contribution. I also serve on the boards of trustees of Alliant International University, where I am a member of the Executive and Finance Committee; and California College of ASU, where I serve as chairman of the Board of Directors. I have also been quite active in my church, Ousley United Methodist Church, having chaired the church council for several years. Although I no longer have that responsibility, I am still involved with the church capital campaign committee and the senior adult ministry. One of my favorite retirement activities is the monthly meeting of the Council of HBCU Past Presidents. A number of former HBCU presidents live in the greater Atlanta metropolitan area. Some were presidents of Georgia colleges and universities, and others like me chose to retire here. Currently there are eighteen members of the council. These women and men have enjoyed distinguished careers, and we are now partnering with the Clark Atlanta University Executive Leadership Institute to help prepare the next generation of college presidents.

I am also spending a good deal of time serving as my wife's business manager and agent. She has always had a passion for art. Unfortunately, a high school art teacher dashed those hopes when he told her that she had no artistic talent. Many young people would never have picked up a brush again after such words coming from the mouth of their teacher. Fortunately for her, she continued to enjoy painting and sketching while pursuing her professional career. Upon retirement she started painting with a new level of commitment and dedication. A pivotal point came while I was serving as the interim president of the University of the District of Columbia. I decided to hang one of her paintings in my office. It was a very colorful figurative piece of art that attracted the attention of everyone who entered the office. At first, I assumed people were just trying to earn a few brownie points with the president by telling him how beautiful the painting was and how talented my wife must be to produce such a piece of art. However, when visitors kept making the same remarks, it became clear to me that I was living with an artist. In fact, I had three offers from members of the staff to purchase the piece. Had they not been employees, I would have sold the painting to the highest bidder. It was at that point that I informed my wife that she needed an agent/manager to sell the art for her. This would allow her to focus on the creative rather than the business side. We agreed that I would do it free of charge. This has led to quite a change in my life, and I enjoy most of what I am doing. Sitting under a tent for three days at an art festival is a challenging and humbling experience. We have been attending art shows and festivals throughout the mid-Atlantic region of the USA. She has also sold paintings and shipped them around the country and abroad. What I have learned is that if you want to be knocked down a peg and have your ego checked, go to an art festival and sit in a tent for three days asking people to "come take a look!"

At most of these festivals I sit or stand out front encouraging passersby to take a look at the art. I have learned a few very important lessons in this new line of work. First, "beautiful art" is really in the eye of the beholder! Some people will look at a piece of art, give you a polite smile, and then walk away. Someone else will look at that same piece and announce that they must buy it immediately and pull out a credit card. There are times when I have encouraged people to buy a particular piece of art for two days, then one individual takes a look at it and says, "I have got to have it!" Lesson two: when you are in an environment with other artists and vendors who, like you, are trying to make money, it forces you to become more assertive as a salesperson. I always tell passersby to "come take a look, there is no charge to look." Most people just look at you and laugh. Once I engage them in conversation, they cannot believe that a former university president is out there "clowning" to get you to look at his wife's art. Lesson three: people are big liars, even more than you would think. If I had five dollars for everyone who has said "I'll be back" and didn't return, we could stop selling art and live on the money from the liars.

This has made me both humble and more aggressive with my sales efforts. For example, on one occasion a man indicated that he wanted to purchase one of our more expensive paintings; however, he indicated that he would have to return the next day and make the purchase because he had a Volkswagen and could not get his father's wheelchair and the painting in the car. Rather than risk never seeing him again, I offered to push my two dogs aside and put the painting in my SUV and follow him home. Much to my surprise he agreed, paid for the painting, and I followed him home. While we lost money and time because of the trip to his home, it was more than covered by the cost of the painting he selected. On another occasion, a woman wanted to purchase two paintings but did not want to carry them around the festival grounds all afternoon. It was a Saturday afternoon, so I agreed to deliver them to her home early Sunday morning if she paid for them. As she pulled out her credit card, she said "As the former president of Jackson State University, I guess I can trust you to deliver them in the morning." Lesson four: people are genuinely impressed by the fact that Joy and I are both former educators. They find it intriguing that two former schoolteachers are traveling around the country selling art. At a pre-Christmas show in Athens, Georgia, I was talking to a woman about buying a piece that she really liked, but she indicated that she did not have the money to make the purchase. An hour later she returned to our area and made the purchase. She said that she told her husband that she liked the art, but almost as important, she wanted to buy it from a schoolteacher like herself.

Finally, I have already mentioned my interest in Latin America, and even in retirement that has not changed. A few years ago, while serving as the interim president of the University of the District of Columbia, my wife and I travelled to Havana, Cuba, to sign a memorandum of understanding between our School of Law and the University of

Havana School of Law. The Obama administration was very sympathetic toward establishing closer ties with Cuba, so our trip was the beginning of what we considered to be a very important first step in establishing a stronger relationship between our two institutions. While there we met a group of graduate students who encouraged me to reach out to other Black students and encourage them to visit Cuba. When I returned to Washington, my plan was to reach out to undergraduate students, especially those who may have an interest in the African diaspora, and arrange study tours to Cuba, Panama, Columbia, Ecuador, and the Dominican Republic. In all these countries there is still visible evidence of the influence of Africa. Unfortunately, the policy toward Cuba has changed, and I was forced to put my plans on hold for the time being.

When I discussed the presidency with my wife nearly thirty-seven years ago, we agreed that there was a life for us after the presidency; but we had no idea that it would be so much fun!

PS: My mother lived long enough to see her dream come true. Each of her three children accomplished what she was never able to do, complete high school. After graduating from high school my brother George entered the military. After graduating from high school my sister Katrina attended a technical school and became a licensed barber. And of course, after graduating from high school, I attended the University of Connecticut.

# ABOUT THE AUTHOR

Photo courtesy of the editor

**James E. Lyons Sr.** is a member of the board of trustees of Alliant International University and chairman of the board at California College of ASU. He has served on the boards of the American Council on Education, the National Association for Equal Opportunity in Higher Education, the National Institutes of Health's Task Force on At-Risk Drinking, and others. He formerly served as secretary of higher education of the state of Maryland and as president of Bowie State University, Jackson State University, California State University, Dominguez Hills, Dillard University, the University of the District of Columbia, and Concordia College Alabama.